HOME LIBRARY

HELPFUL
HOUSEHOLD
HINTS

Contents

Made in the United States of America

ISBN: 0-88176-382-9

Cover Design: Terri Kolodziej

Introduction

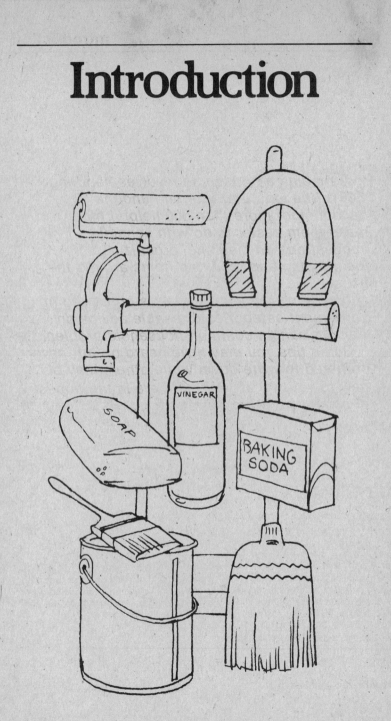

Managing a household involves handling 1,001 little jobs that often go undone. This handbook of more than 500 helpful hints can make them easier to do with sensible suggestions on cleaning, organizing, maintaining and repairing items around the house.

This time-saving reference is organized in convenient categories of usable advice on ways to handle common household problems.

Some tips you may have heard of, but never bothered to write down while others may be new to you. All are offered here in the hopes of making your life easier.

Babies
and Toddlers

Feeding Time

When you take your baby out of his crib for feeding, put a warm heating pad in his spot. Remove the heating pad and when he goes back to bed, the bed will be nice and snuggly warm.

Sometimes it is difficult to spot the ounce marks on baby's bottle in a dimly lit room at 2:00 a.m. To save your eyesight, mark the ounces clearly with nail polish.

Glass marbles in the sterilizer will attract many of the minerals in the water and help keep baby bottles clear of mineral deposits.

With the dishwasher water temperature set at 180 degrees, you can sterilize baby utensils along with the family dishes.

Storing bottle nipples in a cool, dry place will help lengthen their usability.

Some deterioration of the rubber in bottle nipples can be slowed by carefully cleaning them, inside and out, and by an occasional brushing with a salt solution.

Enlarge a bottle nipple's hole by boiling the bottle nipple for about five minutes and then allowing it to cool for about three minutes with toothpicks lodged in the holes. If you later find you have made the holes too large, reboiling the bottle nipples will reduce the size of the holes.

A soft-drink carton makes a tip-proof container for storing baby bottles in the refrigerator.

Feeding Solids

Put a large plastic bag from the cleaners under the high chair to catch the food that surely will end up on the floor.

A towel bar attached to the back of a high chair is convenient for hanging a washcloth and bib.

A muffin pan makes a good warming tray at feeding time. Hot water in the muffin cups keeps food jars warm, and there's even room for a washcloth and sponge. A little baking soda and water on the cloth will combat odors. The muffin tin is easy to hold on your lap, too.

Hold a small kitchen sponge under baby's chin, and you will catch most food dribbles.

Homemade baby food not only costs less but can contain none of the salt, sugar, or other additives that many commercial preparations do. Foods prepared from fresh vegetables retain vitamins that could be lost with exposure to light and aging.

If you put just enough food in the blender to cover the blades one inch, baby's food will be lump free.

An ice-cube tray is an excellent container for freezing blocks of baby food.

When a child is just learning to drink from a cup or glass, make it less slippery by putting several strips of tape around it.

Bathing Your Baby

If your tiny baby is terrified of his bath, bathe him

with you in the adult tub so he can have the security of your body warmth and encircling arms.

Use soap sparingly to preserve baby's own protective skin oils.

Cornstarch has the same protective effect as baby powder. Dust it into your hand (away from the baby) and spread onto the diaper area.

Diaper pins can be kept handy in a "pin cushion" fashioned from a bar of soap. The soap also lubricates the pins so they will go through the diapers more easily. When the soap gets too full of holes, move it to the bath and start a new pin cushion.

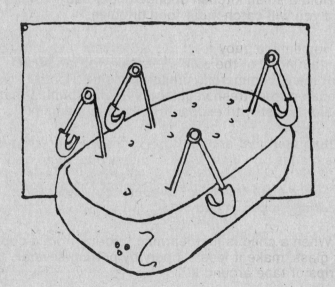

Wear a soft cotton glove on one hand when bathing baby, and you will have a better grip on the wiggly, soapy tyke.

Babies and Toddlers

Install decorative, non-slip tape or cut-outs in your tub or shower to give your toddler a better footing.

Washing Baby Clothes

When washing woolens, be sure both the wash water and rinse water are tepid, as hot water will shrink wool.

Dissolve mothballs in the final rinse water when you are washing woolens to be stored.

Traveling with Children

A small, inflatable pool can double as a traveling playpen or crib.

A large bed sheet provides a clean infant play area on a motel floor or on a grassy area outdoors.

Have an adult ride in the back seat of the car alongside a restrained toddler. The child will be happier and less likely to demand a place up front.

A baby food jar or other small jar with a screw-on cap lets you carry a small, wet cloth in your purse for clean-ups.

If you bring mesh vegetable bags to the beach, when it's time to go, you can bag up all the toys and dunk them so you won't bring home a load of sand.

Refrigerate baby's formula in an insulated cooler packed with ice.

A cookie sheet makes a good traveling lap tray on which kids can color and play games.

Child Care Tips

An easy way to weigh baby is to first weigh yourself. Then step on the scale a second time—with baby. The difference is baby's weight.

Even "ouchless" bandages sometimes pull the skin. To avoid this, rub baby oil over and around the bandage, and it will come off more easily.

Hold a compress of baby oil or olive oil over a splinter for a few minutes, and it will slide out easily.

Hide a hard-to-swallow pill with ice cream, pudding, or applesauce, and it will go down more easily.

When a child graduates from crib to bed, put pillows between the mattress and springs so the bed is higher at the edges. This will help prevent the child from falling off the bed while sleeping.

Olive oil, peanut butter, or cold cream rubbed into chewing gum caught in a child's hair softens the gum for easier removal. If ice is held to the gum to make it brittle, the gum can be broken off the hair.

No Tears

When washing a child's hair, smear cold cream on his eyebrows and eyelids to keep out suds.

Babies and Toddlers

Play Time

Chalkboard paint available at paint stores lets you convert any door or wall into a blackboard.

For a washable eraser, use a large household sponge.

Empty plastic bandage cans with flip tops make good storage containers for crayons.

If you spray shellac on cardboard games, paper dolls, and jigsaw puzzles, they will last longer.

To lift the dents in damaged ping pong balls, boil them.

A play table just the right height for children can be fashioned by cutting off the legs of an adult-sized table.

Cover the edges of swing seats with slit sections of an old garden hose to soften the blow in case the seats swing into a child.

An old shower cap can protect the seat on a bike that must be kept outdoors.

An old tractor or truck tire can see new life as a sandbox enclosure. Inspect it first for any protruding metal bits.

Put plastic bags over mittens when children will be playing in the snow. The mittens will keep their hands warm, and the bags will keep the mittens dry.

Plastic bags used over shoes inside boots will keep both shoes and feet dry in case the boots are not totally waterproof.

Children's overshoes can get mixed up at school. Your child will find the right pair easily if you decorate them uniquely with plastic stickers.

Children's Clothes

Before you go shopping, trace paper patterns of clothing that fits your child, and you can buy without the hassle of a try-on.

Coat hooks installed low enough for children to reach will encourage them to hang up their clothes themselves.

For longer wear, apply iron-on patches to the insides of the knees of jeans.

A nut pick can help loosen the inevitable knots in kid's shoe strings.

Frayed shoelace ends can be tamed by dipping in clear fingernail polish.

If he can see himself, your child may do a better job of grooming. Help him by affixing a mirror at his eye level, perhaps on the back of the bathroom door.

Safety

Your child never should open a door to strangers. Install a second door viewer at the entry door low enough so the child can use it to tell you who's there.

Babies and Toddlers

Sliding glass doors can be made safer with colorful decals positioned at eye level. The decals will alert people that the doors are closed. Don't forget to add some at your child's eye level, too.

If you create your own identifying design with reflective tape, your child not only will be able to find his boots but he also will be safer with the added visibility.

Dogs, Cats, Birds and Fish

Dogs, Cats, Birds and Fish

Pet Toys

Unless you want all your shoes and gloves to be considered fair game, never make a toy of an old shoe or glove.

A ball tied inside an old nylon stocking is less likely to roll under furniture. However, it still bounces and rolls enough to make it a good pet toy.

Feeding Pets

If you open both ends of pet food cans, you will be able to push out the entire contents. This is much easier than digging with a spoon.

The pet's dish won't scoot across the floor during the meal if you put a rubber or vinyl mat underneath. The mat also makes clean-up easier.

Bathing Pets

Keep all cleaning and rinse materials—wet or dry—away from your pet's eyes and ears.

Dry cornmeal is a good dry shampoo for any furry pet. Rub it in well, and then brush it out. Baking soda can be used the same way, and it deodorizes, too.

Put a piece of nylon net over the bathtub drain when bathing pets to catch their hairs before they clog the drain.

Make a special shower curtain to put up at the tub for your dog's bath. Cut holes for your arms and head. Even though you will get splashed, the floor won't.

If you put a rubber or vinyl floor mat in the tub, your pet might feel more secure about its footing and therefore enjoy the bath more.

Laundry bluing added to the bath water for a white pet will make its coat look even whiter.

If you put baking soda in the rinse water, it will make a pet's coat softer and shinier. It also deodorizes.

Some owners of fluffy, long-haired dogs use cosmetic rinses designed to leave human hair tangle-free.

If your pet's hair is tangled with burrs, crush them with a pair of pliers or oil them, and they'll be easier to remove.

New Pet

The old idea of putting a ticking clock in with a young pet really does keep it quiet when left alone.

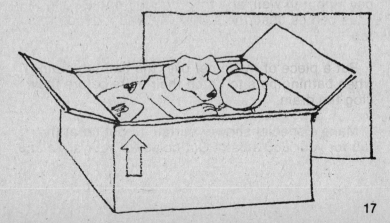

Dogs, Cats, Birds and Fish

A hot water bottle filled with warm water and wrapped in something soft also is good.

A playpen your child has outgrown can see new life as a pet corral. Staple screen wire around the bottom edge so the animal cannot slip through the bars or get its head caught in them.

Outside Pets

Wrap reflective automotive tape in a spiral around your pet's collar so motorists can see it better at night.

So your pet won't be able to knock over its water dish outdoors, use an angel food cake pan as the dish and put the center hole over a stake.

Indoor/outdoor carpet makes a good entrance flap for a dog house because the material will stand up to the weather. Cut it to fit, staple it in place, and slit it. Help your dog through a few times until he understands how to get through on his own.

For the Birds

Pick up spilled or scattered birdseed with damp paper towels.

Fumes from solvents, ammonia, and paint can harm your bird. Think of your pet when you use any of these.

Fish Story

Nylon net or even a hair net over a fish bowl will prevent fish from jumping out.

Solving Pet Problems

Make a cat scratcher by gluing a carpet scrap (backing side out) to the side of a large appliance.

A few mothballs sprinkled under your sofa cushions will discourage your pet from taking over your favorite spot.

A barely damp chamois or wash cloth can be used to remove pet hairs from upholstery.

A slice of raw onion put over a spot where your pet made a mistake will let him know this is not an acceptable place to use again. Leave the onion there a day or so.

Dogs—yours or the neighbors'—can cause havoc with outdoor garbage cans. To make your cans tip-proof, find old auto tires large enough and set the garbage cans inside.

Garbage cans with side handles can be made tipproof another way. Drive a metal pipe into the ground so the top is just higher than a handle. With the handle slipped over the pipe, the garbage won't tip.

Green-Thumb Suggestions

Watering Plants

For dripless watering of a plant in a hanging basket, put a few ice cubes on top of the soil (but not against the plant). The melted water will reach the roots slowly enough to be absorbed, and by then it will be warm, too.

Plants benefit from humidity, which you can increase by grouping plants together. Humidity can be created by putting a layer of pebbles or perlite in a pan with just enough water to cover the bottom of the pan. Place potted plants on top of the pebbles or perlite, and they will be nourished by the constant evaporation of moisture.

It is best to water plants with water that is room temperature. Very cold water can shock some plants.

Many plants do well in the humid atmosphere of a bathroom.

Giving Plants Enough Light

Clean windows will let in more light for sun-loving plants.

Let each plant have its day in the sun with a regular exchange schedule.

Rotate each plant so it won't become lopsided from bending toward the light.

Green-Thumb Suggestions

Keeping Plants Clean

Plants with fur-like leaves should not be washed. Instead, take a soft brush or one of the plant's own leaves and wipe it gently over the plant.

A thick, watercolor brush is a good tool for cleaning the fur-like leaves of African violets.

An old toothbrush is another excellent aid in manicuring plants.

Feeding Plants

You can nourish your plants by feeding them ground eggshells or finely diced banana skin. Work these into the soil and watch your plants flourish.

Vacation Time

Many plants can tend themselves for a few weeks if properly treated before you leave on vacation. To minimize moisture loss, group your well-watered plants on a tray of wet gravel and cover with large, transparent, plastic bags. Make sure the plants are in a cool place out of bright or direct light.

Larger plants can be put in the bathtub on top of bricks. Water the plants and fill the tub with water to the top level of the bricks before covering the plants and tub with clear plastic. Put a table lamp or your bathroom light on a timer to give 12 hours of light a day; make sure the faucet doesn't drip and that your overflow drain works.

Large floor plants can survive uncovered if you water them well before you go and move them out of strong light.

If you run a wick made of soft cotton rope or nylon hose from the soil in a pot to a container of water, your plant will water itself.

Stem Support

Sometimes you can give first aid to a broken stem that is still attached by making a splint with toothpicks and tape.

Use pipe cleaners to tie plants to poles. Dip them first in green food coloring and they won't even show.

Popsicle sticks make good supports for small plants.

Potting Plants

A bottle cap placed crimped edge down makes a good cover for the drainage hole in the bottom of a pot. The cap keeps soil from washing out the hole, yet the crimped cap edge allows just enough room for extra moisture to escape.

A plug of steel wool, a piece of nylon hose, or burlap also can be used to hold the soil but allow drainage in a pot.

Green-Thumb Suggestions

If a plant is top heavy and keeps tipping over, try double-potting it. Put the plant and its original pot inside a larger pot with rocks or gravel between the two.

You don't have to buy commercially packed potting soil to be sure your greenery is planted in insect- and disease-free soil. Instead, dig your own soil and put it into a baking pan or roaster up to a depth of four inches. Cover tightly with heavy aluminum foil and stick a meat thermometer into the middle of the soil. When the temperature reaches 180°F, cook for at least one half hour but do not allow the temperature to go over 200°F. Allow to cool for 24 hours before using.

Discouraging Pests

If your cats are digging in the soft soil around your house plants, discourage them by covering the soil with sharp, white stones. These will serve the dual purpose of reflecting light and making the pot an uncomfortable spot for the cats to play.

If a plant is plagued by bugs or a disease that could spread to other plants, isolate it for treatment. Large, clear, cleaner's bags are good for isolating sick or infested plants.

Sewing Shortcuts

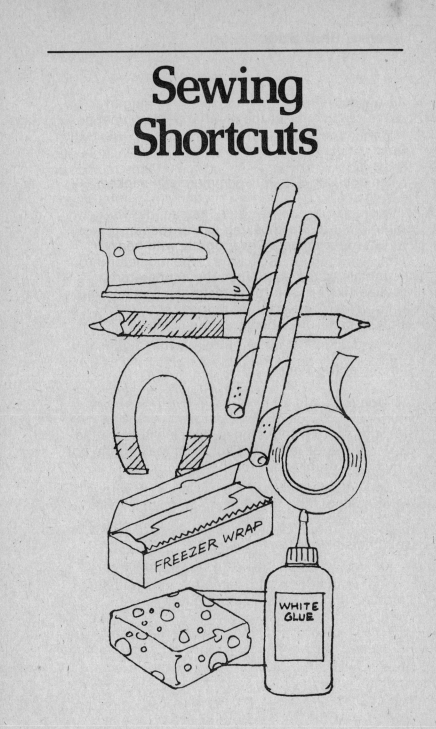

Sewing Shortcuts

Saving Patterns

Patterns wear out after repeated use. Preserve
them with plastic-coated freezer wrap, available at
most grocery stores. Place pattern pieces face down
on the plastic surface and press with a dry iron.

You can give added life to new patterns and
reinforce your favorite old ones with a press-on
backing sold at fabric stores.

Rolling rather than folding makes patterns last
longer. Try rolling yours in a cardboard tube saved
from paper towels or gift wrap.

Press wrinkled pattern pieces with a warm, dry
iron to avoid distorting pattern size.

Interfacing

Whenever possible, use fusible interfacing so
that the two layers of fabric can be handled as one.

Small detail pieces are easier to work with if the
interfacing is first fused in place. Fusibles will
stiffen fabric, so be sure to test for appearance
before using.

Some delicate, lightweight, synthetic fabrics
cannot stand the heat needed to apply a fusible
interfacing. Work with a scrap first.

Thin webs of fusing material can be used to put
up hems, hold appliques in place, or secure patches
before stitching.

Buttons

If you have a loose button on a garment and cannot sew it right away, wrap a piece of transparent tape around the remaining threads to hold the button until it can be sewn on more securely.

Help four-hole buttons stay on longer by sewing them on in two steps. Sew two holes and finish off the other two holes. If one thread comes loose, the other will still hold the button.

Prevent thread tangles when hand sewing by first running the thread through some beeswax.

Slip a matchstick or round toothpick over the face of a shankless button. Work all the stitches over the stick. Before fastening the thread, wind it several times around the thread between the garment and the button. Remove the toothpick.

Buttonholes

If the interfacing shows along the edge of a buttonhole, camouflage it by coloring with a matching pencil or pen.

When slitting machine-made buttonholes, place a pin at each end of the buttonhole, in front of the bartacks, to prevent cutting through the ends.

To get the look and strength of a corded buttonhole without the fuss, try threading two regular threads through the eye of the needle.

Sewing Shortcuts

Zippers

To hold a zipper for machine stitching, use transparent tape instead of hand-basting. After sewing, the tape is easily torn off. Never stitch through the tape.

Self-basting zippers have thin strips of fusible material on each side of the zipper tape to speed up the application. Test on a scrap before using on a delicate fabric.

Regular drafting or transparent tape can be used as a topstitiching guide. Remember not to stitch into the tape and to remove it immediately after stitching.

All zippers should be pre-shrunk before being sewn.

Lubricate a cranky zipper by rubbing the teeth with a bar of soap.

Preventing Puckers

Some fabrics tend to pucker slightly when sewn on a machine. This usually can be prevented if the fabric layers are held taut as they go under the pressure foot.

Another solution is to sandwich the fabric between layers of tissue paper while stitching. This prevents the fabric from puckering and getting caught in the needle hole.

It's a Snap

To match the snaps on a garment closing, rub a piece of chalk on the half of the snap that protrudes. Then close the garment as it will be when worn and press together with your fingers. The chalk will come off and show you exactly where to sew the other half of the snap.

Pick Up

Use a damp sponge mop to pick up sewing threads. This works on carpet as well as on smooth floors.

Spilled steel pins can be picked up with a magnet.

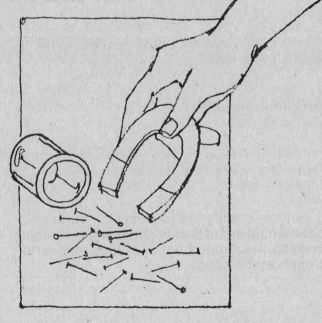

Sewing Shortcuts

Pins and Needles

Large glass- or plastic-head pins tend to break sewing machine needles because the head holds the entire pin too high for the machine foot to go over easily.

Replace sewing machine needles often because dull or bent needles can cause skipped stitches or damaged fabrics.

When you sew leather or leather-like fabrics, use special leather needles with a sharp, wedge point.

If you have long fingernails and find using a regular thimble difficult, try one with an open end. You get protection where you need it, and it doesn't interfere with your nails.

Narrow strips of fusible web can be used to hold hems in place. Test fuse on a scrap of fabric to see if the fused web will be invisible on the right side.

Press the hem fold with a strip of paper between the fabric layers to prevent an impression on the right side of the garment.

Instead of basting or pinning the hem, use broad, flat hair clips to hold the hem in place. Just measure the width of the hem and slip on the hair clips.

Fabric glue can be used in place of pins or basting. Apply a light coat of glue, press with your fingers and allow to dry.

Patch Work

Worn out purses or gloves can provide fashionable leather for elbows on sweaters or jackets.

When you need to put a patch or emblem on a garment, be sure it's on straight and in the right position. Before sewing, put a bit of white glue or fusible web on it and stick it to the garment. Then you can sew it by either hand or machine and know it is in the right position.

Laundry

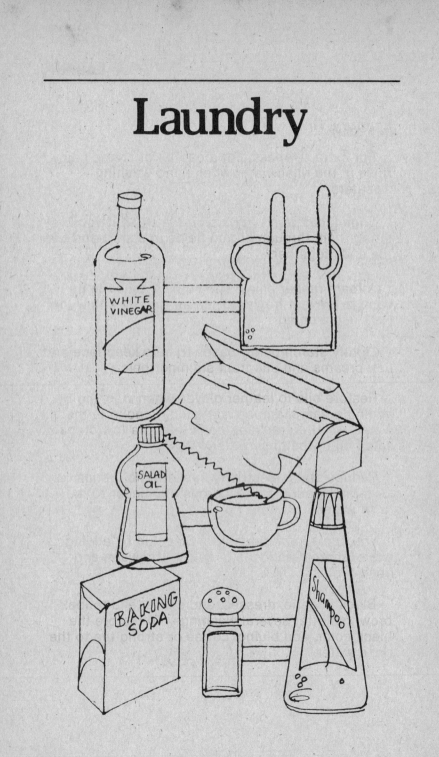

Laundry Tips

For extra softness, put a capfull of creme hair rinse in the rinse water when hand washing sweaters.

Shoe laces won't get lost in the wash if you first string them through button holes in a shirt and tie the ends together.

A foam rubber pillow should be washed in its case to prevent fraying. Then air dry the pillow (do NOT use a dryer).

Lightly starch pillow cases to help keep face and hair creams and oils from staining them.

Restore oils to leather gloves when washing by adding a hair shampoo containing lanolin to the water. An alternate method is to add a few drops of salad oil to the rinse water.

Reduce static electricity in synthetic fabrics or curtains by adding a few drops of vinegar to the rinse water.

You can keep fabrics from bleeding by adding two or three teaspoons of salt to the wash and rinse cycles.

Black lingerie, dresses, and shirts tend to look brownish after several washings. To restore the black color, add bluing, coffee or strong tea to the rinse water.

Spots and Stains

Perspiration stains will come out of clothing if the garments are soaked in salt water before laundering.

Another way to remove perspiration stains is to apply a paste of baking soda and allow this to sit for a while.

Mildew spots can be removed from white fabrics by rubbing with a mixture of lemon juice and salt. Place the fabric in the sun to dry before washing.

Grease spots on cotton garments can be treated with salad oil. Rub the oil into the grease and then wash in hot, sudsy water.

Treat grease and grime on shirt collars and cuffs by rubbing in a thick coat of chalk. Allow this to sit overnight, and launder as usual.

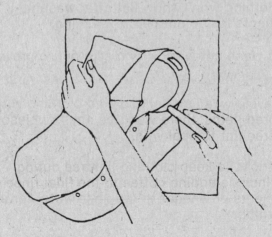

Pencil marks around shirt pockets should be erased before washing because they are more difficult to remove once wet.

Make-up can be taken out of dark clothing by rubbing it with bread.

Washing Whites

Get white socks clean by soaking them in washing soda before washing to help loosen the dirt.

Enjoy truly white handkerchiefs again by adding a touch of cream of tartar to the wash water.

To prevent nylon from turning yellow, pre-soak in a baking-powder solution.

Avoiding Lint

Dark clothing won't show lint after washing if you turn garments inside out before washing.

Always wash corduroy wrong side out to prevent lint from sticking to it.

If you avoid washing dark-colored clothing with light-colored items, there won't be any troublesome, light-colored lint to deal with.

Other tricks to keep clothing lint-free during washing include adding coffee to the final rinse of dark garments or vinegar to the rinse water for any color clothing.

Suds Away

Suds will dissipate quickly if you sprinkle salt over them. This is a way to banish suds from a sink so you can rinse, or to clear suds from a washing machine that overflowed because of an overabundance of soap.

You can remove all soap from clothing by adding a cup of white vinegar to the washer's final rinse water. For hand washing add a proportionately smaller amount of vinegar to the rinse.

Tennis Shoes and Sneakers

New tennis shoes can be sprayed with starch to keep dirt from getting embedded.

Bleach tennis shoes ultra white by adding lemon juice to the final rinse.

A soap-filled scouring pad is effective for cleaning sneakers.

Plastics

Add several ounces of glycerin to the rinse water when washing plastic items such as shower curtains, baby pants, or draperies to keep them soft and pliable.

Preserving Pleats

After you wash a permanently pleated skirt, gather the pleats together tightly and carefully slip a nylon stocking down over the skirt. Hang it up to dry, and your pleats will look freshly pressed.

Line Drying

Keep heavily starched clothes from sticking to a clothesline by covering it with a strip of wax paper before hanging the clothes.

When using a wire coat hanger to drip dry clothes, cover any rust spots with clear fingernail polish to avoid spotting the clothes.

Similarly, protect drip-dry clothing on a painted coat hanger by covering the hanger with a towel or aluminum foil.

Pressing and Ironing

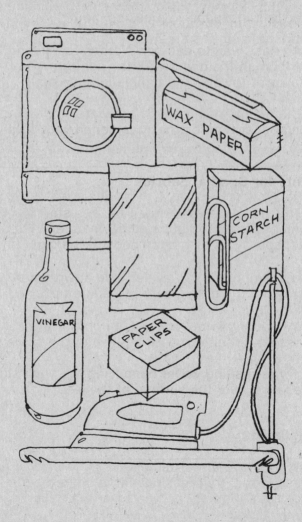

Pressing and Ironing

Make it Easy

A collapsible, clamp-on holder will keep the iron's cord out of your way and up off the clothes while pressing.

A piece of lightweight muslin or batiste makes a good and inexpensive pressing cloth.

An easy way to dampen clothes for ironing is to put them in the dryer (with the heat turned off), add a few wet towels, and tumble until damp.

Clothes dampened with hot water will be ready to iron sooner than clothes dampened with cold water.

Hints for Special Fabrics

The shiny look of chintz can be restored by ironing the fabric right side down on a piece of waxpaper. This also adds body to the chintz.

Iron embroidery or eyelet face down on a thick towel and the embroidery will stand up.

You also can revive velvet or corduroy by pressing it face down on a piece of the same fabric.

Try refreshing velvet by moving the back side of the fabric over the surface of the iron.

Synthetics

If you have unwanted creases in a permanent press fabric, try pressing with a cloth moistened with a solution of two parts water and one part white vinegar.

Pressing and Ironing

Acrylic knits stretch out of shape if moved when wet and warm. Since they darken when steam-pressed, allow them to return to normal color (meaning the material has dried completely) before moving them on the ironing board.

Prevent seam impressions from showing on the right side of your permanent press clothing by ironing with paper strips placed under seams. Cut your strips from brown paper bags.

Using Your Iron

If your iron is sticky from ironing starched clothes, run it across a piece of aluminum foil, fine sand paper or paper sprinkled with salt. Avoid salt or any other abrasive if your iron is Teflon coated.

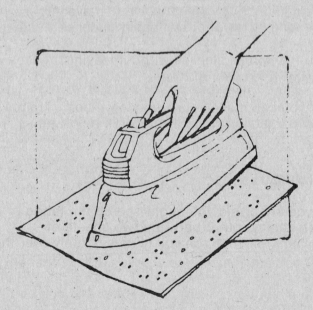

For smoother ironing, frequently run your iron over a white candle or paraffin wax. Be sure to wipe the ironing surface on a clean cloth or a paper towel before ironing again.

Water from defrosting the refrigerator or from the air conditioner condensor won't corrode the insides of a steam iron, as tap water will.

Wash-and-wear garments should be "touched up" on the wrong side to prevent shine.

Pleats and Sleeves

Hold pleats in place with paper clips when ironing.

Sometimes when pleats are pressed, the folds leave marks on the pleats above. To avoid these, place long strips of brown paper under each pleat.

You can press sleeves without leaving creases if you slip in a rolled up towel.

Or you can make your own sleeve board from a heavy cardboard tube covered with a soft fabric.

Scorch Marks

If you are afraid you might scorch the fabric you're ironing, put it between two sheets of aluminum foil. The iron will glide smoothly over the foil.

Pressing and Ironing

Scorched spots on woolens can be removed by wetting the spot, rubbing in cornstarch, and brushing when dry.

Scorched cotton should be put immediately in cold water and left to soak for 24 hours. Often the scorched area will then be gone.

Energy Saver

If you use a dry iron rather than a steam iron, cover your ironing board with heavy-duty aluminum foil and put the cover over this. The aluminum will reflect the heat back to the garment you're ironing, speeding your work and saving energy.

Cooking
Hints

Cooking Hints

Useful Kitchen Hints

If you're separating eggs, and some yolk slips in with the egg whites, scoop it out with the eggshell. The shell acts like a magnet to draw out the yolk.

Use your egg slicer or cabbage grater for slicing mushrooms.

Don't wash strawberries until you're ready to use them. They keep better dry.

Too much salt in the soup or stew? Add a raw potato and boil for 5 minutes. When you remove the potato, the salty taste will be gone.

A slice of bread in the cookie jar will help keep cookies moist. Change the bread every other day, and use it for toast.

Keep your brown sugar soft by storing it in an air tight jar. Add a slice of grapefruit, orange, or lemon peel, and when the peel dries out, substitute another. Fruit peel also can be used to soften already hard sugar.

Another way to soften hard brown sugar is to heat the oven to 350 degrees, turn it off, put the brown sugar in a container in the oven, and close the door. As soon as the sugar warms, it will be soft again.

A piece of white bread can be used to remove the scorched taste from rice. Put the bread on top of the rice, replace the pan's lid, and wait for a few minutes. The scorched taste should be gone.

Time and Work Savers

Sprinkle a little salt in a frying pan before you start cooking to keep grease from splattering.

The last bit of ketchup or dressing will slide easily out of a bottle that has been sitting in a pan of hot water.

There will be no waste when you measure syrup, molasses, or honey if you first dip the measuring cup in flour. Sticky mixtures will pour out completely and instantly.

Keep your salt free-flowing in damp weather by keeping the shaker on the stove. Its warmth will keep salt dry.

A roll of adding machine tape kept in a dispenser in the kitchen is just right for making grocery lists.

Thicken gravy quickly by adding instant mashed potatoes instead of flour to your water.

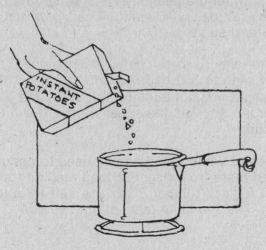

Cooking Hints

Tenderize a tough roast by cooking it with tomatoes. The acid in the tomatoes breaks down the tough fibers in the meat. This works using either fresh or canned tomatoes.

After you have fried foods such as onion rings, potatoes, or fish, you can clean your lard and shortening for re-use. Cool the grease, add water, and heat until it's almost boiling. As this mixture cools, most food particles and residue will sink to the bottom. Refrigerate the mixture until solid. The remaining particles will rise to the top and can be scraped off. (This will not work on oil.)

If you have trouble getting a whole ham out of the can without breaking it, put the can in hot water before opening. The heat will melt the gelatin next to the can, and the ham will slide out easily.

Remove whole asparagus from a can without ruining the tips by opening the bottom of the can and pulling the asparagus out bottom first.

Keep an avocado from turning dark after peeling by giving it an air-tight wrapping. Put the pit back in the hole and wrap the whole avocado in plastic. Store in the refrigerator.

Keep potatoes fresh longer by scraping off sprouts as they appear.

Kitchen
Helpers

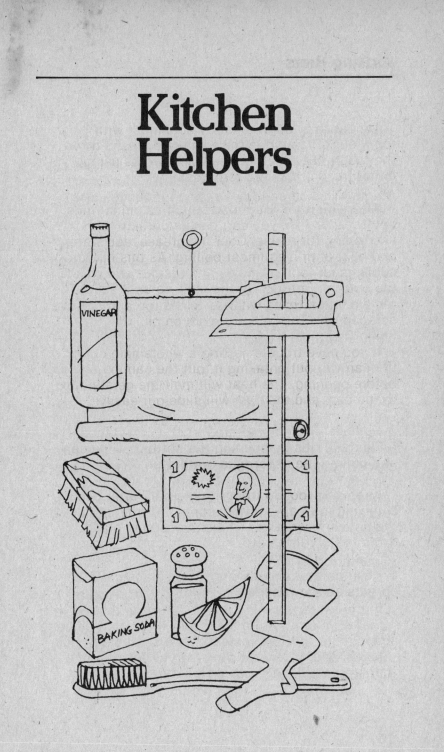

Kitchen Helpers

Handy Protectors

To protect your hands when polishing silver, slip plastic bags over them and secure with rubber bands. This same trick keeps your hands clean when painting.

Protect your hands from the cold when rearranging frozen foods in the freezer by wearing kitchen mitts—they protect against cold as well as heat.

Adhesive Shelf Paper

If you have trouble with bubbles and creases when applying adhesive-backed paper to shelves or drawers, use a blackboard eraser to smooth them out.

An iron is a useful tool when removing adhesive-backed paper. Put a towel over the paper and press on top of the towel. The warmth will help the adhesive release its hold, and the paper can be pulled up easily.

Countertop Stains

Stains on a laminated plastic countertop are difficult to remove and never should be rubbed with steel wool or abrasive cleansers that could damage the counter further. Instead, try a solution of milk, bleach, and water, allowing it to sit for only one minute and rinsing with water immediately.

It's the Berries

Plastic berry baskets stapled to the pantry wall or the inside of a cabinet door can hold small packages of sauce mixes, seasonings, and cold drink mixes.

Fight Grease Splatters

Protect the wall behind your stove from grease splatters by installing a washable vinyl shade on the wall behind the stove. Position it upside down so the roller is hidden by the stove. When cooking, pull the shade up and fasten it to a hook several feet above the stove; when you are finished, roll the shade down out of sight.

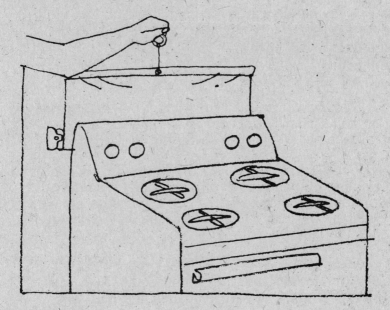

Kitchen Helpers

The Refrigerator

Though no one may ever know whether you clean behind your refrigerator, you should face up to the task. Dust that collects on the coils at the rear of the refrigerator can cut down on its efficiency and shorten the life of your unit.

Check that your refrigerator is level. If it is not, it may be working harder than it needs to and wasting energy.

For most efficient operation, the freezer compartment should be kept fairly full with items placed close together. The refrigerator portion, however, works best with spaces left to allow air to circulate.

If you notice water standing in the bottom of the refrigerator, there may be an air leak around the door. To test the gasket, close the door on a dollar bill. If the bill can be pulled out easily, the gasket needs to be replaced.

Remove lint and dirt from under the refrigerator or any similar narrow space with a yardstick wrapped in an old nylon stocking.

A few drops of vanilla extract diluted in a cup of water and then rubbed on a refrigerator's interior surfaces eliminates odors. Some homemakers also keep a cotton ball soaked with the extract inside the unit at all times.

Make a fresh tray of ice cubes more quickly by leaving three or four cubes in the tray when you refill it. The already frozen cubes help cool the fresh water.

Pots, Pans, and Utensils

Dark stains in aluminum pans often can be removed by boiling water containing about one tablespoon of cream of tartar per quart.

Never leave or store food in aluminum containers because it could pit the metal.

Copper can be made shiny if rubbed with a lemon wedge dipped in salt. The lemon also could be dipped in a paste of salt and vinegar, or the copper could be rubbed with silver polish. Whichever method you use always wash well.

Sour milk cleans copper. Pour some in a flat dish and soak the copper for an hour; clean as usual.

A generous coat of baking soda barely moistened with water and left overnight will help remove burned-on foods.

Running cold water over the bottom of a hot pan in which food has burned also will loosen food particles.

Use newspaper to wipe excess grease from a pan before cleaning.

You can prevent sticking in a skillet by sprinkling the pan with salt and then warming the utensil in the oven for five minutes. Remove the pan, wipe out the salt, and use as usual.

A cast-iron skillet will not rust if you wipe all surfaces of the dry but still-warm pan with a little cooking oil.

Kitchen Helpers

Let the blender clean itself. Fill it less than halfway with hot water, add a few drops of dishwashing liquid, cover, and run for ten seconds. Rinse and dry.

A toothbrush makes a handy tool for cleaning the cutter mechanism on a can opener or the beaters on a mixer.

If your can opener, mixer, or other food-handling device requires lubrication, use cooking oil and there will be no chance of oily tasting food.

The Dishwasher

If your automatic dishwasher leaves a film on your dishes, set a bowl containing two cups of white vinegar in the bottom rack and run the load through another wash and rinse cycle. If filming persists, change brands of automatic dishwasher detergent.

A dishwasher's hot water and detergent can harm bone-, antique- or wooden-handled cutlery and other wooden objects, so you should clean these by hand in warm, mild suds.

Cleaning the Whole House

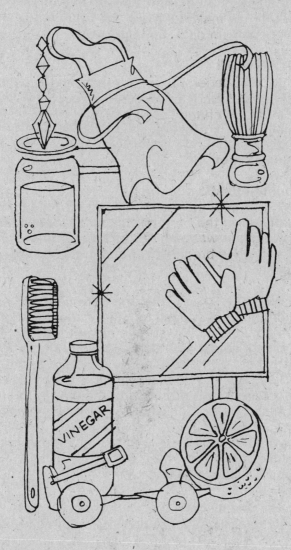

Cleaning the Whole House

Keeping Yourself Clean

You can fashion an efficient cleaning apron from a compartmented shoe bag by attaching strings to the bag and filling the pockets with rags, polishes, brushes, and other lightweight supplies.

Taking Measures

You can formulate correct dilutions of cleaning compounds every time if you use a bucket marked to indicate quarts and gallons. Lines can be drawn inside the pail with red fingernail polish.

Names and Buttons

A toothbrush can be used to clean between push buttons or around raised-letter trade names on stoves, refrigerators, washers and dryers or other appliances.

Get the Picture

One of the dangers of cleaning picture glass with liquid cleaners is the chance for moisture to get under the glass and spoil the print or photo. Use a dry procedure to avoid this; dust the glass and then polish it with tissues designed to clean eyeglasses.

Mirrors can be cleaned with a cloth dipped in a solution of borax and water. Or, use a cloth saturated with denatured alcohol.

To clean deeply carved picture frames, use a clean, dry, plastic squeeze bottle. Pump the bottle and it will act as a small bellows, blowing dust out of the tiny crevices.

* A tarnished gilt frame will shine again if cleaned with a rag dampened with turpentine.

Light House Cleaning

It is easy to clean a crystal chandelier without even taking it down. Fill a glass or jar with a mix that is three parts water and one part denatured alcohol. Then spread a pad of newspapers under the fixture to catch drips, climb a ladder to the chandelier, and submerge each pendant in the glass. The pendants will sparkle as they drip dry.

Crystal pendants also can be cleaned with an ammonia and water mixture. Put on an old pair of cotton gloves, dip your hands in the liquid, and rub the crystal.

Vacuum Cleaner Cleaning

Empty your reuseable vacuum cleaner bag onto a dampened newspaper to avoid having dust fly.

Prevent flying dust when changing disposable vacuum cleaner bags by placing a dampened newspaper over the bag opening.

A torn reuseable vacuum cleaner bag can be mended by pressing iron-on patches over any holes.

*WARNING: When using a flammable liquid avoid inhaling fumes by providing adequate ventilation. Never work near a flame or spark-creating flame device.

Cleaning the Whole House

You can unclog your vacuum cleaner hose with a straightened coat hanger. Leave a small hook on the end of the hanger and push or pull out any debris plugging the hose. Test that the hose is clear by dropping a coin down it. If the coin falls freely through the length of the hose, you will know all debris has been removed.

When you are finished dusting the floors, vacuum the dust from the mop by holding it under the vacuum hose. Dust and lint can be removed from brooms this way, too.

Work Saver

Clear plastic stapled on the inside of louvered closet doors will help keep out dust and moths.

Wheels for Heavies

To save your back when you want to rearrange heavy furniture, lift one end at a time and slide a child's roller skate or skateboard under each end. Then wheel away the furniture.

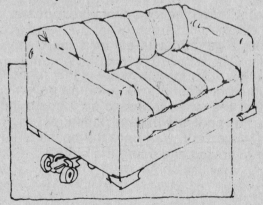

Cleaning Challenges

Knickknacks can be washed faster than they can be dusted. Just swish them in water containing a little liquid detergent, rinse, and drain on a towel. If you are in a real rush, speed-dry them with a hand-held hair dryer.

If you have a weekend mechanic or handyperson around the house, wrap the door knobs with a rag so you won't have to clean greasy or oily fingermarks from the door and woodwork.

Clean door knobs without ruining the finish on the door by cutting cardboard shields to go around the knobs and key plates.

Clean your ruffled or pleated lamp shades with an old shaving brush or baby's hair brush. The bristles are so soft they won't snag or harm the fabric.

Dusters

A paint brush makes an excellent duster. Flick it along door jambs, around windows, and in corners difficult to get into with a dust cloth.

Suitable dusting rags actually can be made from any old cloth. Pour a little furniture polish into a glass jar and swish it around so it coats the whole inside. Pour out any excess polish, put the cloth in the jar, cover, and wait until the polish is absorbed before removing and using the cloth.

Cleaning the Whole House

Make a duster from a piece of cheesecloth by dipping it in a solution of two cups of hot water and one-quarter cup of lemon oil. Allow the cloth to dry, and you will have an effective dust cloth.

Clean Smells

Give your room a pleasant scent by dabbing perfume on the cool bulb in your lamp. As the bulb gets hot, a sweet smell will permeate the air.

You can clear smoke from a room quickly by dampening a towel with diluted vinegar and waving it throughout the room.

Furniture Fuzz

Animal hair can be removed from furniture with a damp sponge or pieces of adhesive tape.

Cleaning Metals

A piece of alum in a silverware drawer will slow the tarnishing process.

Sometimes it is easier to use a sponge than a cloth to clean silver because a sponge can squeeze into many crevices a cloth cannot.

Pewter becomes lustrous when rubbed with fine steel wool. (Fine steel wool won't scratch the pewter.) Follow the rubbing treatment with rinsing and drying.

A truly unusual way to clean pewter is to rub it with cabbage leaves.

Copper and brass articles can be cleaned by rubbing with a lemon dipped in salt. Wash them with water and dry with a soft cloth.

To retard tarnish on polished brass, rub with a cloth moistened with olive oil.

Defrosting

If your refrigerator is defrosted by allowing water to drip into the tray under the freezer compartment, don't risk spilling the water on the way to the sink. Instead, leave it there, and allow it to refreeze. Once the water is frozen, remove the tray and let the frozen chunk melt in the sink.

To make defrosting easier, rub the insides of the freezing compartment with shortening, or spray with a commercial coating designed to keep food from sticking to pans. The ice will slip right off the next time you defrost.

The Dropped Egg

To clean raw egg dropped on the floor, sprinkle salt over it and allow it to sit for 15 to 20 minutes. Then, simply sweep up with a broom.

Fake Flowers

Clean sturdy artificial flowers by placing them in a large paper bag containing cornmeal or salt. Shake, and the cornmeal or salt will act as an abrasive to remove the dust.

Cleaning the Whole House

Candle Holders

Silver candlesticks that have wax dripped on them can be cleaned unharmed if you put them in the freezer first. After the wax freezes, it will peel off easily.

Fireplaces

* Stubborn smoke stains can be cleaned from a fireplace by washing with a solution of TSP (trisodium phosphate) and water. (Mix one-half cup of TSP with one gallon of water, and be sure to wear gloves.)

Alternative methods of removing smoke include rubbing it with an art gum eraser or applying a paste of cream of tarter and water. Allow the paste to dry, and brush it off.

*WARNING: When using a flammable liquid avoid inhaling fumes by providing adequate ventilation. Never work near a flame or spark-creating flame device.

Odor
Controls

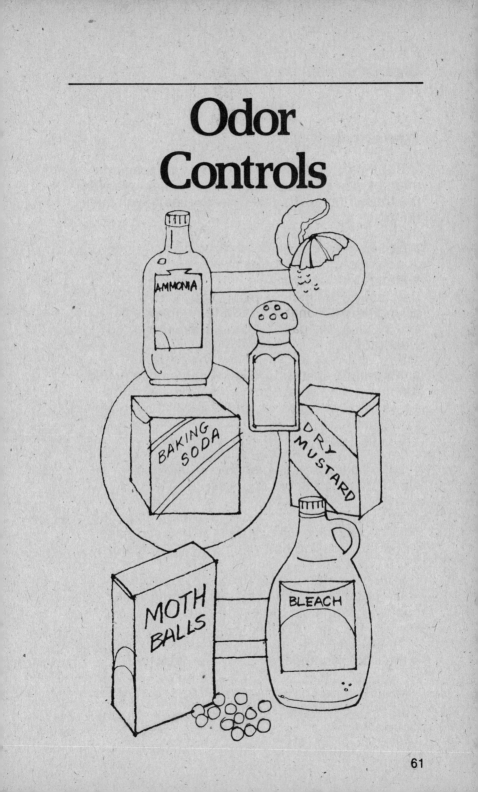

Odor Controls

Whole House Scents

Sprinkle cinnamon on a sheet of aluminum foil and put it in a hot oven, leaving the door open. As the cinnamon heats, it will make the house smell good.

The kitchen can be deodorized by putting a spoonful of ground coffee in a container and heating it in the oven.

Or, boil water containing a little ammonia.

If you put a solid room deodorizer next to the air-return vent of a forced-air heating system, the fresh smell will be carried through the ducts into every room.

Fighting Cooking Odors

Salt rubbed into a wooden cutting board eliminates food odors and also lifts stains.

Any pot, pan, or container that has a lingering odor should be washed with a baking soda and water solution. Or, boil vinegar in the container.

If you don't have time to clean stove or oven spills or boil-overs immediately, minimize their odors by sprinkling them with salt.

To sweeten a sour-smelling waste disposer, feed it the rind of orange, grapefruit or lemon.

A tablespoon of borax or baking soda are good food waste disposer deodorizers.

Other odor-banishers for sinks include a strong salt water solution or a cup of laundry bleach.

The refrigerator can be kept odor-free if you leave in it an open box of baking soda, a few charcoal briquettes in a dish, or a lemon half.

If an odor persists in a freezer or refrigerator, empty the compartment and clean all surfaces with club soda or a baking soda and water solution.

Strong odors that stay on your hands, such as fish smells or onion odors, can be removed if you wet your hands and then sprinkle on baking soda. Work the soda over your skin, and then rinse away the soda—and the odor.

Mothballs in the bottom of a garbage can will help minimize odors.

Odor Controls

The Sweet-Smelling Home

A dish of vinegar placed in a room full of cigarette or cigar smokers will help freshen the air.

After a party attended by heavy smokers, leave a dish of ammonia in the smoky rooms overnight to remove the stale odor.

Clean and sweeten ash trays by washing them in baking soda and water, mixed one tablespoon to the quart.

The odor of fresh paint can be removed in a day by leaving in the room either a dish of ammonia, vinegar or sliced onion in a bowl of water.

An unwrapped bar of soap will keep a drawer or linen closet smelling pleasant.

Odors coming from a central air conditioner usually indicate a fungus in the condensate drain. Pour laundry bleach into the condensate pan; it will kill the fungus and leave the system odorless.

Deodorize bottles by filling them with a solution of dry mustard diluted in water and allowing this to stand overnight. The next morning, wash and dry your odor-free bottles.

Mice and Insects

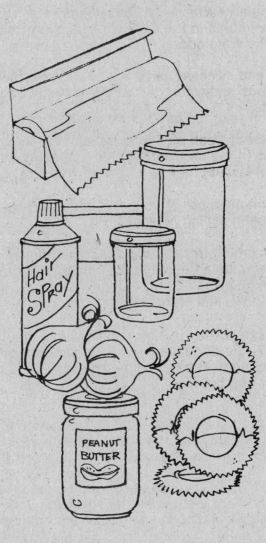

Mice and Insects

Mice

Peanut butter makes a good bait for a mousetrap.

If you don't know where mice get in, sprinkle some flour or talcum powder in likely areas and look for tracks.

Pack steel wool tightly into the wall openings around pipes to discourage the entry of mice.

Close all floor drains to prevent mice from climbing in from the sewers.

Wasps

Aerial nests sometimes can be covered with a heavy plastic bag. Insert a pesticide strip before closing the bag.

Spray nests at dusk since that's when the entire clan will be there.

For the Birds

Shiny Christmas tree ornaments will spin in the breeze and keep birds away, too.

Strips of aluminum foil hanging from a string across your garden will move with the slightest breeze and scare away birds.

Clusters of tin can lids tied together and suspended from a string stretched across your garden, also will discourage birds from visiting.

When a bird lands on the string to case your vegetables, he'll cause the lids to clang together, and the noise will scare him away.

Artificial snakes will keep birds out of fruit trees. Some people even wrap sections of old garden hose around tree limbs and get the same results.

Pantry Pests

Insects often enter the house with groceries, transfer foods from boxes or paper packages to airtight containers made of glass or plastic.

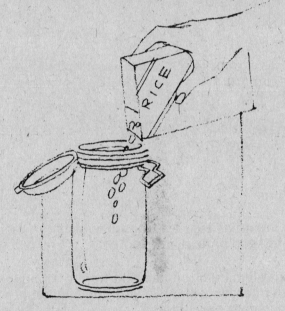

Garden Pests

Intermingle onions and garlic in your garden, and the odor will drive away many bugs.

Mice and Insects

Snails and slugs can be controlled by leaving a flat dish of stale beer level with the ground before sunset. Early the next morning, you'll find the dish full of the creatures.

Bugs in Paint

Mix a tablespoon of citronella into a gallon of paint to repel insects that might otherwise get stuck in your paint job.

Stains

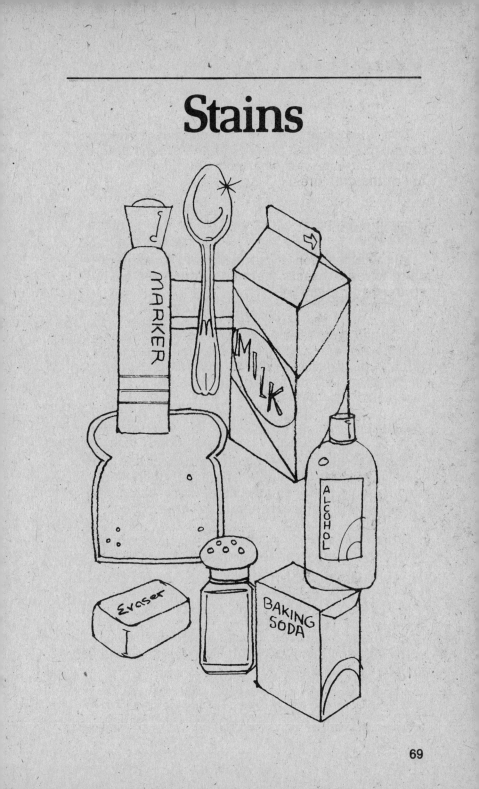

Carpets and Upholstery

Acid

If acid gets on your carpet, immediately dilute with water and then neutralize the acid. Baking soda and water or club soda not only neutralize, but also dilute.

Alcoholic Beverages

Quickly wipe up alcohol spills on carpets or upholstery and dilute right away with cold water so the alcohol doesn't have time to attack dyes. If the drink is wine, there may be a stain problem. See "Wine."

Blood

* Dampen a blood stain with cold water and then apply carpet or upholstery shampoo. Follow that treatment with dry cleaner fluid. If you use an ice cube to dampen carpet, you won't over-soak it.

Add a tablespoon of table salt to a cup of cold water to dampen and loosen blood stains.

Butter

* Cornmeal or ground, dried corn cobs absorb greasy stains such as butter. Dry cleaning fluid can be used to lift these stains, too.

*WARNING: When using a flammable liquid avoid inhaling fumes by providing adequate ventilation. Never work near a flame or spark-creating flame device.

Candle Wax

Place an ice cube in a plastic bag and hold it against the wax. The wax becomes brittle and then can be chipped away with a dull knife.

Place a blotter over the wax spot and press with a warm iron. The blotter will absorb the melted wax. Remember to keep moving the blotter so it doesn't get over-saturated and stop absorbing.

Chewing Gum

The ice-cube-in-a-plastic-bag treatment used to remove candle wax also will make gum brittle enough for removal with a dull knife.

Coffee

Blot coffee stains quickly and then dilute with plain water.

Crayon

* Sometimes the iron-and-blotter treatment that works for candle wax is effective on crayon, but the best removal substance is dry cleaning fluid.

*WARNING: When using a flammable liquid avoid inhaling fumes by providing adequate ventilation. Never work near a flame or spark-creating flame device.

Stains

Grease

* Scrape up as much of the spilled grease as possible and then apply a dry cleaning fluid.

* Rub with paint thinner and then cover with salt.

   Cornmeal absorbs and lifts grease from carpets and upholstery. Leave overnight and vacuum.

Ink

* Ball-point pen ink (except red ink) can be lifted with hair spray, other inks respond to dry cleaning fluid.

   Sprinkle salt on ink, and as soon as some ink is absorbed, brush the salt away and sprinkle again.

Mildew

* Try removing mildew with white vinegar, but if the mildew spots remain, dry cleaning fluid is a reliable alternative treatment. In any case, get rid of moist conditions or the mildew will return.

Mud

   Allow mud to dry; then softly brush (to loosen) and vacuum.

*WARNING: When using a flammable liquid avoid inhaling fumes by providing adequate ventilation. Never work near a flame or spark-creating flame device.

Paint

* Wet latex paint responds to water and oil-base paints to turpentine (absorb the turpentine with cornmeal after applying). Follow these treatments with a dry cleaner or shampoo.

Pet Stains

Blot pet stains from carpet or upholstery and then clean with club soda. This only works satisfactorily, however, on fresh stains.

Equal parts of white vinegar and water will clean pet stains from your furnishings.

Soot

Sprinkle a generous layer of table salt over soot, allow it to sit for a while, and then vacuum up both the salt and soot.

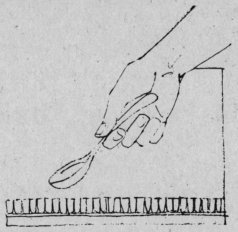

*WARNING: When using a flammable liquid avoid inhaling fumes by providing adequate ventilation. Never work near a flame or spark-creating flame device.

Carpet Color

If the spot or the remedy changes a carpet's color, you might be able to touch up small places with artist's acrylic paint.

Felt markers are available in many colors and you might be able to match your fabric or carpet to disguise a blemish. If you use permanent ink markers to replace lost color, go slowly.

Tar

* To remove tar, use dry cleaning fluid sparingly and blot frequently during treatment.

Wine

Wipe up quickly. Dilute; then clean the spot immediately with cold water. You can dilute red wine with white wine and then clean with cold water. Cover the area with table salt, wait ten minutes, and vacuum.

Stains on Other Fabrics

Blood

Use only cold water on blood spots as hot water sets the stain.

*WARNING: When using a flammable liquid avoid inhaling fumes by providing adequate ventilation. Never work near a flame or spark-creating flame device.

Cover a dampened blood spot with a generous coat of dry starch. Allow the fabric to dry and brush away the starch—and the spot.

A paste of meat tenderizer and cold water will lift a blood stain.

If ammonia won't hurt the fabric, soak blood stains in a solution of one tablespoon of ammonia per pint of water.

Chocolate

Remove chocolate or cocoa stains by soaking thoroughly with club soda before washing.

Rub talcum powder into chocolate stains to absorb them.

Milk will keep chocolate stains from setting. Apply the milk as soon as the stain occurs.

Chocolate stains can be removed by rubbing shortening into them and then laundering.

Egg

Soak egg stains in cold water for an hour or so before laundering. Hot water will set egg stains.

Fruit

Pour a mixture of detergent and boiling water through the fabric to remove fruit stains.

Stains

Grass

Grass stains sometimes respond to rubbing on denatured alcohol or a diluted solution of ammonia applied before laundering. Lard rubbed into grass stains removes them.

Water Marks

Water marks on clothing usually will disappear if rubbed with the rounded back of a silver spoon.

Grease

Cornstarch absorbs grease from fabrics, as does talcum.

Salt dissolved in ammonia often is an effective grease remover.

Ink

An ink stain can be treated by soaking overnight in sour milk or buttermilk. Speed the milk's action by rubbing salt into the spot.

Lemon juice may erase an ink stain.

Hair spray often will lift a ball-point ink stain, unless it's been made with red ink.

Lipstick

Lipstick can be removed by rubbing the stained area with a slice of white bread.

* A little petroleum jelly applied to a lipstick smear helps it to respond better to a dry cleaning solution.

Dab salad oil on lipstick and launder after about five minutes.

Mildew

Soak badly mildewed clothing in buttermilk overnight, and then launder as usual.

Exposure to sunshine can also rid clothing of mildew.

Vinegar does away with some mildew, while dry cleaning or laundering usually is effective for removing mildew from clothing.

Mud

Remove mud spots by rubbing with a slice of raw potato.

*WARNING: When using a flammable liquid avoid inhaling fumes by providing adequate ventilation. Never work near a flame or spark-creating flame device.

Stains

Nail Polish

If a fabric won't be damaged by nail polish remover, you can use it to lift nail polish spots, preferably from the underside of the fabric.

Scorch Marks

An onion slice can be used to treat scorch marks. Rub with the onion and then soak in cold water before laundering.

An old-fashioned way of removing scorch marks is to rub a damped slice of stale white bread over the area.

Hydrogen peroxide will bleach out scorch spots, but be careful because it may also affect fabric dyes. Test on an inconspicuous area before using on the scorched area.

Shoe Polish

Treat shoe polish on clothing with rubbing alcohol.

Add a tablespoon of borax powder to the wash to fight marks left by shoe polish.

Soot

Erase soot from clothes with an artgum eraser.

Leave dry salt on a soot spot for a while and later you can use a stiff brush to remove both the salt and soot.

Tar

Shortening left on a tar spot for about ten minutes will soften it so it can be scraped away before washing.

Furniture Upkeep

Scratches

Some scratches can be hidden with paste furniture wax or oil furniture polish.

* On natural wood or antique finishes, polish with one part turpentine mixed with one part boiled linseed oil. Apply with a clean, soft damp cloth.

Rub a walnut or pecan nut meat over scratches. The oil often will hide a scratch.

Iodine camouflages scratches on some furniture. Test it first on the underside. If the iodine is too dark, add denatured alcohol; if it is too light, expose the iodine to the air before using and it will darken.

Match Scratch

If furniture or woodwork sports a scratch made by a match, the mark can be removed by rubbing with a lemon wedge.

White Spots

Toothpaste rubbed on with a damp cloth will remove white rings made by wet glasses. Try it on other surface stains, too.

White marks also can be removed by rubbing with any mild abrasive or oil. Abrasives could include ashes, salt, soda, or pumice; suitable oils are olive oil, petroleum jelly, cooking oil, or lemon oil furniture polish.

*WARNING: When using a flammable liquid avoid inhaling fumes by providing adequate ventilation. Never work near a flame or spark-creating flame device.

Furniture Upkeep

Often a coat of petroleum jelly or cooking oil left for 24 hours will lift white spots.

Rubbing white spots with paste furniture polish often will remove rings.

First Aid for Furniture

Clear transparent tape applied over a snag on a rattan chair will keep clothes and stockings from catching and being ruined. Also, the tape barely will show.

Or, dab over the spot with clear nail polish.

Put thumbtacks into the bottom ends of wooden chair legs so they slide more easily.

If a furniture leg caster becomes loose, tighten it by wrapping a rubber band around the caster stem and reinserting it.

A wobbly chair can be steadied by putting a block of wood putty under the short leg. Form the putty to fit, and, when dry, stain it to match.

Use thread as packing around a chair rung before re-gluing it.

A piece of paper that is stuck to a polished table can be lifted after saturating the paper in cooking oil.

Cleaning and Polishing

A rag soaked in left-over tea can be used to clean varnished furniture.

While you are waxing the furniture, wax the insides of ash trays, too. This makes them easier to clean.

* Wax and dirt build-up on furniture can be removed with mineral spirits paint thinner. Apply with one rag and remove with a clean one.

Wear cotton gloves while polishing furniture to avoid leaving fingerprints.

After you have polished your furniture, sprinkle on a little cornstarch and rub to a high gloss. The cornstarch absorbs any oil and leaves a highly polished surface free of fingerprints.

Stripping and Refinishing

* When using paint stripper on furniture with legs, put tin cans under each leg to catch the stripper as it drips down. Not only does this help protect the floor, but you can reuse this excess.

Before you varnish furniture in a house with central heat, turn off the system so there is less dust circulating.

Brown paste-type shoe polish gives an interesting stain and finish to unfinished furniture. Apply, let dry, and buff.

Strong tea also is a good stain for unfinished furniture.

*WARNING: When using a flammable liquid avoid inhaling fumes by providing adequate ventilation. Never work near a flame or spark-creating flame device.

Furniture Upkeep

Bed-Lam

Squeaky bed springs can be silenced with a coat of spray wax.

If the noise is caused by the springs touching the frame, pad the frame with pieces of sponge.

If bed slats continually fall out, slip wide rubber bands over the ends of the slats and they won't move so easily.

Drawers

Prevent drips when painting drawers by taking the drawers out and painting them standing face up.

Lubricate the slides of a wooden drawer with a bar of soap, a candle stub, or a rag sprinkled with dry starch.

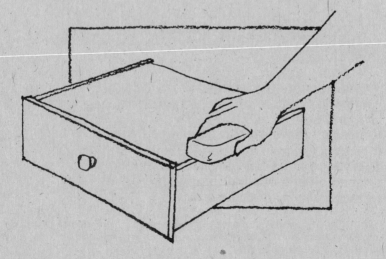

If you have a drawer that won't open all the way because something inside is sticking up, slip in a kitchen spatula to push down the wayward item.

Upholstery

If you put upholstery scraps in an envelope and staple it to the bottom of the newly covered piece, you will have them later for patching.

Cut foam rubber upholstery padding with your electric carving knife.

Hammer decorative furniture tacks without damaging the heads by placing a wooden spool against the tack. You will hammer the spool, not the tack.

When using ornamental tacks for upholstery, tack extras into the frame in an inconspicuous spot so you will have a replacement if needed.

Covering plastic kitchen chair seats is easier if you warm the plastic first. A heating pad can be used for this.

Leather

Leather furniture can be cleaned with stale beer.

If you're not a beer lover, try a mixture of one pint linseed oil and one-half pint water. Combine the two in a quart jar and shake well.

Furniture Upkeep

Wicker

If your wicker furniture has become wobbly, wash it outdoors with hot soapy water. Then rinse with a hose and allow the furniture to air dry. The wood and canes will shrink and tighten.

Saggy wicker or cane seats also will tighten if treated with hot water. Vinegar added to the water freshens the wicker or cane.

Metal Furniture

Keep rust from forming on chrome kitchen chairs by coating them with wax.

Decal Removal

Decals can be taken off painted furniture by soaking them with vinegar.

The Bathroom

The Bathroom

Cleaning the Tub

In most cases, a ball or pad of nylon net is abrasive enough to clean bathtub rings without using cleansers.

A capful of mild liquid dishwashing detergent added to bathwater will let you enjoy a bubble bath and will prevent a ring too.

Treat stubborn tub stains with a paste of cream of tartar and hydrogen peroxide. By the time the paste dries, the stains should be gone.

A paste made of borax powder and lemon juice can be used to rub away rust stains on a tub.

Bath Mats

You can clean rubber or vinyl bathtub mats by tossing them into the washer along with a few bath towels. The terry cloth scrubs the mat, and all come clean. Some shower curtains also can be cleaned this way.

Shower Heads

Vinegar will loosen stubborn mineral deposits from a shower head. Remove the head, take it apart, and soak it in vinegar. Then brush the deposits loose with an old toothbrush and clean the holes by poking with wire, a pin, or an ice pick.

Shower Curtains

Don't throw away your old shower curtain; just put the new one on the same hooks, but on the outside. The old curtain will get all the water and soap scum while the new one stays clean.

Plastic shower curtains will stay soft and flexible after cleaning if you add a few drops of mineral oil to the rinse water.

Or, keep them soft by wiping occasionally with a warm-water, mineral oil solution.

A few extra shower curtain hooks hung on the rod can be used to hold a back brush, a net bag for bath toys, or each family member's wash cloth.

Grout

Laundry bleach can be used to remove mildew from grout.

When all else fails to freshen white grout, cover it with white, liquid shoe polish. Any polish that gets on the tiles can be wiped away with a rag when it dries.

A white fingernail pencil also will cover stained grout.

Soap Savers

For a soap saver, slit a sponge to hold slivers of soap. Wet and squeeze the sponge, and suds will appear.

A sock filled with soap slivers makes another good substitute for a sudsy wash cloth.

Tile Walls

Before you start cleaning the bathroom, run the shower at the hottest water temperature. The steam will help loosen dirt throughout the room.

A sponge mop makes quick work of cleaning a shower wall.

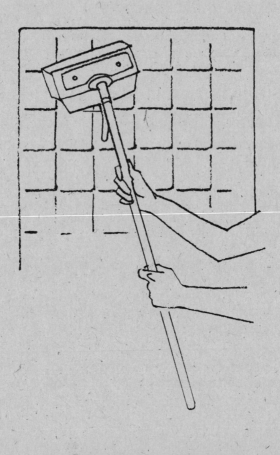

Soap scum on dry ceramic bath tile can be removed by rubbing with dry steel wool. Wash the wall normally afterwards.

Keep your cleanser handy and clean the tub or shower just after you bathe before the scum has a chance to harden.

If you also wipe shower walls with a towel after each shower, you rarely will have to clean the walls. This also prevents mildew from getting started.

Furniture polish or furniture wax applied to clean ceramic tile walls will keep soap film from accumulating. (Don't treat ceramic tile floors this way, however, as they would become dangerously slippery.)

Mirror, Mirror

An old nylon stocking is an excellent "cloth" for cleaning and polishing a bathroom mirror.

Spray a coat of shellac on the back of a bathroom mirror to seal out moisture, which eventually can damage the mirror.

Rubbing alcohol will remove a hair-spray haze from a bathroom mirror.

A light film of glycerin will keep steam from fogging a bathroom mirror.

The Bathroom

Porcelain Stain

Rust stains under a toilet bowl rim can be removed with full-strength laundry bleach. Truly stubborn stains can be rubbed off with a very fine steel wool or wet-dry sandpaper, available at a hardware store.

Bathroom Organizers

Use cup hooks to hang toothbrushes on the wall or under a cabinet.

Glue small magnets inside the medicine cabinet to hold nail files, cuticle scissors, clippers, and other small metal objects.

A paper towel rack in the bathroom will keep paper towels handy for bathroom clean up and will save regular towels when hands are really grimy.

Blotters used as shelf paper in medicine cabinets will catch medicine or cosmetic spills.

An extra slot in the toothbrush holder can keep a spoon handy for taking medicines.

Clean toothbrush holder grooves with cotton swabs dipped in vinegar.

Bathroom Window

A window can be frosted for privacy by brushing on a mixture of four tablespoons of epsom salts and a half pint of stale beer. The result will be opaque glass.

Opaque stained glass pieces, silver Mylar or wax paper also could be glued to windows for privacy.

Or, cover a window with mirrored squares. These not only block an outsider's vision, but they also make a small bath look larger.

Floorings

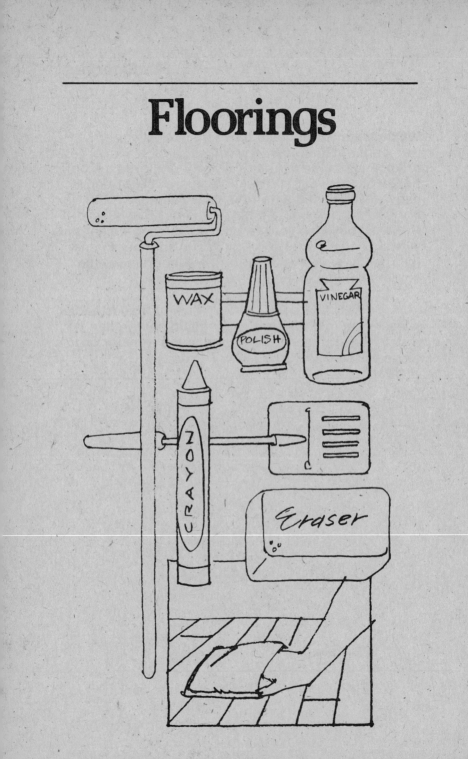

Waxing and Cleaning Floors

Apply paste wax to the floor with a glove-type pot holder or workman's glove. These are very strong, easy to clean, and sure save your hands.

Wash your highly waxed floors between waxings with a solution of one cup of fabric softener in one-half pail of water. This mixture will not remove the shine, and it smells good, too.

Instead of waxing your floors on your hands and knees, stand and use a long-handled paint roller. It also is easy to reach the floor under a radiator or stove with a paint roller.

Floorings

To remove wax from a linoleum or tile floor, mop with a solution of three parts water to one part alcohol. The floor will be clean and ready for new wax.

Add a little vinegar to the mop bucket when cleaning a kitchen floor. The vinegar helps the detergent remove cooking grease particles that have settled out of the air.

Marks on Resilient Flooring

Remove black marks made by shoe heels by erasing them with a pencil eraser. This usually will not harm the wax.

A damp rag containing silver polish or toothpaste will lift crayon marks from vinyl or linoleum.

Remove scuff marks and dirt from a well-waxed floor with fine, dry steel wool. This will not remove the shine, as damp mopping will.

Spills on waxed linoleum can be cleaned up with milk instead of water, as the milk will not ruin the wax.

Dents and Other Damage

Dents in a floor often can be filled with clear nail polish or clear shellac. Because the color will show through, dents won't show.

To remove a bulge or tame a loose seam in a

linoleum floor, place a piece of aluminum foil over it and run an iron over the bulge several times. (The heat will soften and reactivate the adhesive.) Put weights over the area to hold it down until cooled.

To patch a gouge, take a scrap of the flooring and grate it with your food grater. Mix the resulting dust with white glue, and fill the hole. The patch should blend well.

You might be able to mend resilient flooring with crayon wax. Find a crayon to match the floor, melt it, fill any holes, smooth the repair, and then wax the floor; the holes should be camouflaged.

Wooden Floors

Sweep talcum powder into the cracks between hardwood floor boards to stop a squeak. The talc acts as a lubricant and keeps the wood from rubbing. Liquid wax, liquid soap, or thinned glue also can silence squeaky floors.

Clean varnished wooden floors with cold tea.

Even after paint is touch-dry on a floor, it can still take foot impressions ... but not if you put down runners of wax paper for a few days.

Carpets and Rugs

If you spot a loose carpet thread, don't pull it or you may unravel part of the carpet. Snip the thread level with the carpet pile.

Floorings

If a burn is all the way to the backing, snip out the charred fibers and put white glue in the opening. Then snip fibers from a scrap or inconspicuous piece of carpet (perhaps in a closet), and, as the glue gets tacky, poke the fibers into place.

A burn in the carpet doesn't have to be hidden with furniture. If the burn is not down to the backing, probably all you need to do is snip off the charred part with fingernail scissors.

Depressions left in carpets by heavy furniture will come up if steamed. Hold an iron closely enough for the steam to reach the carpet, but don't allow the iron to actually touch the fibers. Rub a coin over the fibers, and they'll stand up again.

If you rotate your rugs so you change the areas of wear, they'll last longer.

Rearranging the furniture can alter sections of wear and tear, too.

Throw rugs won't slip out from under you if you put strips of double-faced carpet tape under the corners.

Wall Repairs

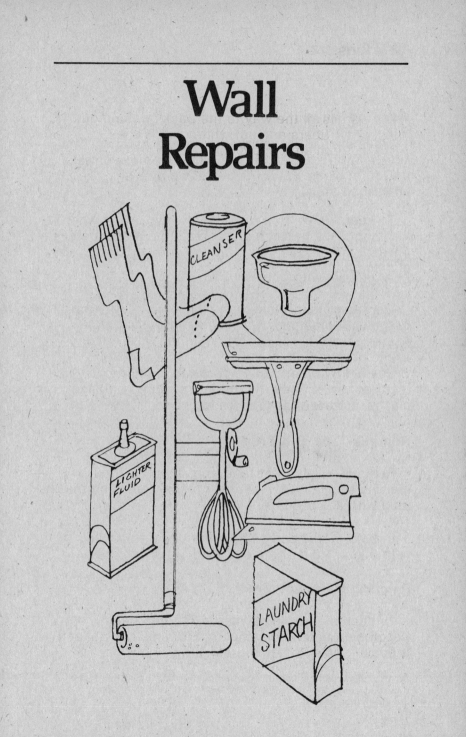

Wall Repairs

Washing Walls

Walls should be washed from the bottom up. This keeps you from creating the hard-to-remove streaks that form when water trickles down over an unwashed area.

To keep water from running down your arm when washing walls, fashion a bracelet from a sponge or a washcloth and fasten it around your wrist with an elastic band.

If you use thick suds when washing walls, you won't need a lot of water and you'll minimize drips. Create a maximum amount of suds with your egg beater.

Use old nylon or banlon socks to clean roughly textured walls. They will not leave behind bits and pieces, as a sponge or cloth might.

Remove Tape and Crayon

Remove transparent tape from a wall without marring the paint or wallpaper by first pressing the tape with a warm iron.

* Crayon marks can be taken off a painted wall with lighter fluid or mineral spirits paint thinner.

Patching Holes and Cracks

Kitchen cleansing powder mixed into paint becomes a patching compound for small holes, and it doesn't have to be painted, either.

*WARNING: When using a flammable liquid avoid inhaling fumes by providing adequate ventilation. Never work near a flame or spark-creating flame device.

Papier-mache can be used to patch wall cracks.

White glue mixed with shredded facial tissue makes a patching substance. Knead the tissue with the glue, adding glue and tissue until the mix is putty-like in consistency.

Fill small holes with white glue squirted straight from the bottle.

Patch hairline cracks with a runny paste made of equal parts of table salt and laundry starch powder mixed with water. Apply it with a small artist's brush or a putty knife.

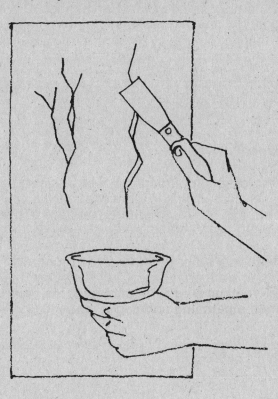

Wall Repairs

Slow down the hardening process of plaster or wall-patching compound by substituting vinegar for about one-fourth of the water required for mixing.

Plaster will also harden more slowly if you mix sugar in with the compound.

Salt added to these mixes will hasten the hardening process.

What to Mix It In

Since batches of wall patch usually are small, you could use the lid of a sauce pan as a "bowl". The handle allows you to easily hold the container during application. Just be sure to rinse out the lid before the compound hardens.

A plunger or half of a hollow rubber ball are other easy-to-hold containers.

Wallpaper

A drop of food coloring in white or clear wallpaper paste gives it a tint that allows you to see more easily exactly where you have applied the paste.

A clean, dry paint roller is a good tool for smoothing wallpaper. If you put the roller on a long handle, you can reach the ceiling or the tops of walls without having to climb a ladder.

A short-napped paint roller can be used to spread wallpaper paste quickly.

A squeegee is a good implement for smoothing bubbles and wrinkles out of vinyl wallcoverings.

When papering over wall anchors or places in a wall where you would like to re-hang shelves or pictures, insert toothpicks in the holes left by screws or picture hooks. As you paper these sections of the walls, force the toothpick points through the paper to mark the places for reinstalling the screws or hooks.

Grease spots that cannot be removed from walls can be sealed with clear nail polish or shellac to keep the grease from soaking through your new wallpaper.

Soak old wallpaper with very hot water applied with a paint roller. If the paper is foil or vinyl-coated, you will have to score the surface so the water can penetrate to the backing.

If you add a small amount of detergent to the hot water, it will soak the wallpaper better.

Many attractive wallcoverings are "stripable," which means that when it is time to remove them, all you have to do is lift a corner and strip off an entire panel simply by pulling on it. The small amount of adhesive residue left on the wall easily can be rubbed off.

Cleaning Wallpaper

If you have a grease spot on non-washable wallpaper, put a blotter over the spot and press it with a moderately hot iron. The blotter will soak up most of the grease.

Wall Repairs

Talcum powder will remove grease spots from wallpaper, too. Using a powder puff, dust the spot well with powder, leave it for an hour, and brush it away. Repeat the dusting if necessary.

A paste made of cornstarch and water will safely lift grease stains from wallpaper.

Or, rub dry borax powder over spots.

Use an artgum eraser to gently rub away soil.

Gently rub fine-grade steel wool over crayon marks on wallpaper.

Repairing Wallpaper

If you need to make a patch for a damaged section of wallpaper, tear the patch from the roll rather than cut it. The less-defined torn edges will blend better with the paper already on the wall, and the patch will be less visible than it would be if cut.

To smooth down a seam that has come loose, smooth it with the back of a spoon. If you don't have any wallpaper paste, white glue makes a good substitute.

Other Wall Coverings

If you want to carpet a wall, apply peel-and-stick carpet squares or affix broadloom with double-faced carpet tape. Double-faced tape also can be used to hold up heavy wallpaper.

Walls can be covered with fabric by stapling or gluing it to the walls or shirring it on drapery rods installed at the floor and ceiling. Bedsheets will give you the most yardage for your money.

Wall Hangings

Hanging Pictures

There's a better method than trial-and-error for positioning a picture hook exactly where you want it on the wall. Instead of guessing, make a paper pattern of the picture (or mirror or wall hanging). Put the pattern over the picture's back side. Pull up taut the wire the picture will hang from. Mark the V point on the paper pattern, adjust the pattern on the wall, and poke through it to mark the wire's V point on the wall. Nail the hook here and your picture will be exactly where you wanted it.

Another method is to hold up the picture by the wire and decide where you want it on the wall. Then, wet your fingertip and press it on the wall to mark the wire's V. The fingerprint mark will stay wet just long enough for you to drive a nail.

To prevent a plaster wall from crumbling when you drive a nail into it, first form an X with two strips of masking or transparent tape over the nail spot.

When the picture wire will show (for example, if you hang a picture from molding), nylon fishing line makes a strong and nearly invisible substitute.

Keeping Pictures Straight

Masking tape wound around the wire on either side of a picture hook will keep a picture from slipping on its wire and becoming crooked.

Two nails placed slightly apart will help a picture hang straighter than it would on just one nail.

Wall Hangings

A picture will remain straight if the wire is looped before being hung on the hook. If it is difficult to make a loop, try hanging the wire with the picture facing the wall and then turning it around to face you. A loop will have been made automatically.

Squares of double-faced tape placed on the back of a picture at the two bottom corners will keep small pictures hanging straight. Position the picture and press against the wall.

If you don't have double-faced tape, make two loops with masking tape, sticky side out, and apply to each of the lower corners. Press against the wall.

Pictures Leave an Imprint

Pictures that have been hanging for some time usually leave a darkish outline on the wall when removed. This can be prevented by allowing better air circulation behind the picture. Leave air space by holding the picture away from the wall with thumb tacks in the back of the frame. Or, use small tabs of self-sticking foam weather stripping.

Picture Groupings

An attractive arrangement of pictures can best be achieved if you first try out various possibilities on the floor. Spread a large sheet of wrapping paper or several newspapers on the floor and experiment with your pictures there. When you hit on a pleasing grouping, outline the frames on the paper, tape the paper to the wall, and drive the hooks through the paper into the wall. Remove the paper and hang your pictures.

When it's time to paint the wall, leave the hooks in place and paint around them. You can then duplicate the exact picture grouping.

Fixing a Loose Frame

If a wooden frame is loose, you might not have to dismantle it for re-gluing. Align the corners on something you already are sure is square, such as the corner of a magazine or piece of paper. Then use a staple gun on each corner of the frame, making sure that the staple spans the joint.

Mirrors

When hanging a mirror with screws that go through mounting holes in the glass, don't tighten them all the way. Leave enough play so the mirror won't crack if there is any shifting in the wall.

Try to avoid hanging mirrors in places where they will receive direct sunlight. The backing on some mirrors might be adversely affected.

Wall Anchors

A tightly rolled metal tube, such as the ones some glues come in, is handy as a masonry or plaster wall anchor. Tap the roll into a small hole and insert a screw for hanging.

Or, taper a dowel and drive it into a hole in a masonry wall. It will secure a screw for hang-ups.

Wall Hangings

When you use a toggle bolt, insert a washer under the head of the bolt. Otherwise, since the hole you must drill usually is larger than the head, there is a danger that the entire bolt may slip into the wall cavity before you get your hang-up in place.

Locating Wall Studs

Heavy objects can be hung without special anchors if you can insert nails or screws directly into the wooden studs behind the walls. But how do you find the studs? One way is to tap the wall gently with a hammer or your knuckles. The wall will sound hollow between the studs but solid if you are tapping directly on top of a stud.

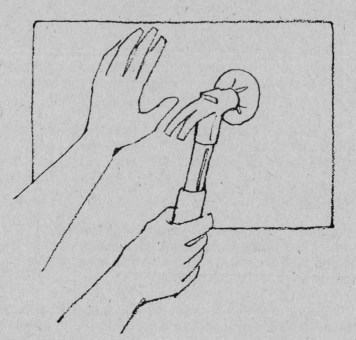

Another method involves using an electric razor. Turn on the razor and move it along the wall. You will notice a different tone when you come to a stud.

A magnet sometimes can be used to locate studs, too. If nails have been used to attach wallboard to the studs, a magnet will show you where.

Bookshelves

Because an accumulation of books can weigh a substantial amount, it is important that bookshelves be securely anchored. Affix them directly into the wall studs or use toggle bolts on plaster or composition board walls.

Doors and Windows

Viewers

Children old enough to answer the door should be able to see who is there, just as you do. Install a second door viewer (peep hole) low enough for your children to use.

Locks

Lubricate a door lock with graphite from a soft pencil. Rub the key across the pencil, put the key in the lock, and move it in and out several times.

Sticking Doors

When a door drags on the floor, the situation can be corrected without removing the door to plane the bottom. Put sandpaper on the floor and move the door back and forth over the abrasive. Add paper or magazines under the sandpaper when it needs to be raised to make contact.

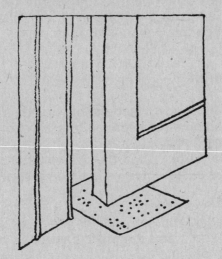

Doors and Windows

Hinges

If you quiet a squeaky hinge by lubricating the hinge pin with a light coat of petroleum jelly instead of oil, you won't need to worry about drips on your floors.

Loose hinge screws can be wrapped with steel wool and reinserted to hold the door securely.

Spare Keys

Never "hide" a spare key in a mailbox, under the door mat, or on a ledge. Instead, wrap the key in foil or put it in a 35mm film can, and bury it where you can easily find it when needed.

Sliding Glass Doors

A decal applied at eye level on a sliding glass door will alert everyone that the door is closed. A clear door is too easily mistaken for an open door, resulting in people walking into the pane.

Doing Windows

A team of window washers, one inside and one outside, works better because missed spots or streaks can be remedied at once. If one person uses vertical strokes and the other uses horizontal strokes, it is easy to see which side a spot or streak is on.

Pure vinegar will remove even the most stubborn hard-water spots and therefore can aid in cleaning windows that have been splashed on the outside by water from a sprinkler.

A well-washed cotton tee shirt or old diapers will give a nice shine to window glass.

* Kerosene makes a good cleaner for glass windows. (Do not, however, use it on any other type of window.) To clean glass windows, mix two cups kerosene and one gallon of warm water, and rub on the solution with a soft rag to remove any built-up soot or cooking grease. Finish by wiping the window with a clean towel. The window will sparkle, and when it rains or water from the hose hits the window, drops will bead up just as they do on a highly waxed car.

The spray bottle attachment that fits on the end of a garden hose lets you clean upstairs glass windows outside without using a ladder. Use automatic dishwasher detergent, and you'll leave only a few water spots.

Don't wash windows in direct sunlight because the sun will dry the cleaner before you get a chance to shine them. Cloudy days are better for washing windows because your cleaning solution will dry more slowly.

An old auto wiper blade can see new use as a squeegee for window cleaning.

*WARNING: When using a flammable liquid avoid inhaling fumes by providing adequate ventilation. Never work near a flame or spark-creating flame device.

Doors and Windows

Removing Putty

Old putty can be removed more easily if first softened with heat. A soldering iron, propane torch, or, sometimes, even a hand-held hair dryer can do the job.

Hard, stubborn window putty can be softened enough to be scraped away if you brush linseed oil over it.

Shady Problems

A shade with too much tension can be tamed by removing it from the bracket and unrolling it by hand two or three revolutions. When it is replaced, it will be less tense.

A shade that won't lift properly needs more tension. Remove it and roll it up two or three revolutions before reinstalling it.

Try using an artgum eraser or wallpaper cleaner to banish window shade spots.

Never oil a window shade mechanism. The oil will soak through the wood roller and ruin your shade.

Pane Pains

A pellet gun hole in a window pane can be filled with clear nail polish or shellac. Dab at the hole, and when the application dries, dab again. Reapply until the hole is filled, and the pane will appear clear.

Stained glass can be fixed the same way with transparent nail polish.

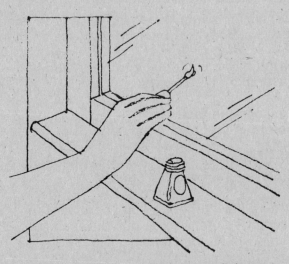

A crack in a window pane doesn't have to spread. Score a small arced line with a glass cutter just beyond the crack. Usually, the crack will travel only as far as the arc.

Window Sills

Protect your window sills by keeping them waxed. Rain spatters and dirt will be easier to wipe off.

Venetian Blinds

If you are interrupted while cleaning Venetian blinds, clasp a clothespin on the last slat you have cleaned so later you will know exactly where you left off.

Doors and Windows

Wear cotton gloves when you wash blinds. Your fingers can rub the slats better than any brush.

Another way to clean Venetian blinds is to hang them from a clothesline and turn the hose on them.

The bathtub is a good place to clean blinds. Rinse them under the shower.

To help keep the tapes from shrinking, rehang blinds before the tapes are fully dry.

White tapes that have yellowed can be made white again with liquid shoe polish.

To install a new Venetian blind cord, sew the end of the new to the old. As you pull out the old cord, the new one will be pulled into place.

Curtains and Draperies

Wire solder or plastic covered wire can be inserted into drapery hems to keep folds in position. After the draperies are hung, bend the solder into desired shapes.

Slip a piece of aluminum foil or a thimble over the end of a curtain rod so it won't snag when it is slipped through the curtain.

Old keys make good drapery weights.

Screen Test

A small hole in a window screen can be closed with dabs of clear fingernail polish. Keep dabbing until the hole is closed, but use only thin coats to avoid drips.

Window Raisers

When a window becomes difficult to raise, rub a candle stub, a piece of paraffin or a bar of soap in the tracks as a lubricant.

Tool
Care

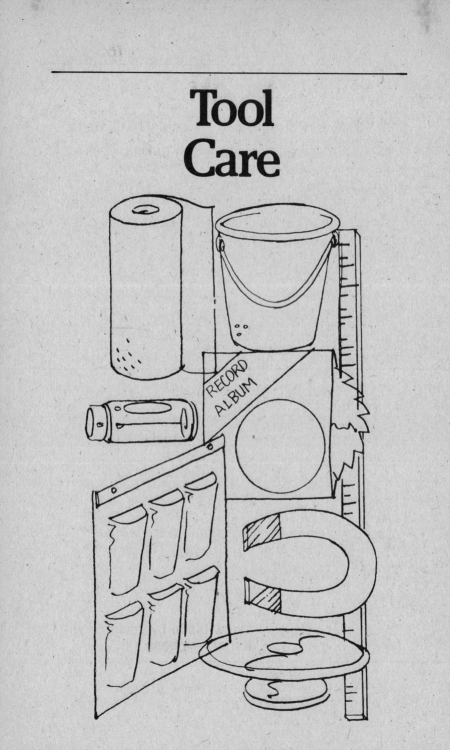

Tool Box

If you are shy of space in which to keep your tools, try stashing them in a kitchen bread box.

Keep a few mothballs in with your tools to help retard moisture and therefore prevent rust. If rust spots do appear, rub them away with a typewriter eraser.

If you don't have a tool box, a large plastic bucket will keep all your tools together and be easy to carry around, too.

Cleaner Hands

Need a hand cleaner in the shop? An aerosol can of shaving cream lets you clean without water. In fact, if you put a thin coat of the cream on before starting a messy task, no dirt or grease will get into your pores.

* Turpentine sprayed from a bottle can be used to clean your hands.

Pump-top jars meant to dispense mustard or syrups are ideal for applying heavy grease.

Saw Tips

Protect the teeth of a saw blade by covering with a length of garden hose that has been slit.

---

*WARNING: When using a flammable liquid avoid inhaling fumes by providing adequate ventilation. Never work near a flame or spark-creating flame device.

Tool Care

Protect circular blades with wide rubber bands cut from an inner tube.

Record album covers are excellent holders for storing circular blades or sandpaper. Line them up neatly in a regular record rack.

Lubricate a handsaw blade by running a bar of soap or a candle stub over the sides.

Screwdriver Holder

Plastic berry baskets nailed to the shop wall can hold screwdrivers slipped through the mesh.

Easy Pick Up

A magnet can be used to pick up a spilled batch of iron nails, screws, or tacks. If you first cover the magnet with a paper towel, the hardware can easily be collected by gathering the corners of the toweling over the pieces and pulling the towel away from the magnet.

Hang-Ups for Liquids

A pocketed shoe bag makes a good holder for items such as shop liquids. It can hold more things in less space than a shelf.

No Lost Tools

Pick an unusual, bright color and paint it on all your tool handles. Your tools will be easy to identify or find if they have been borrowed or simply left in the wrong place.

A Light Touch

Tape a penlight to the top of your power drill for better visibility.

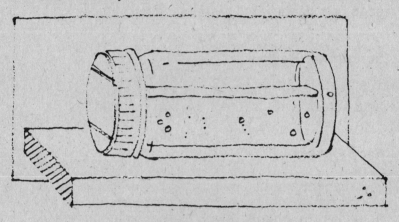

On the Level

If you don't have a level, take any tall, straight sided jar with a lid and fill it three-quarters full with water. Lay the jar on its side and when the water is level your surface is flat.

Measure Up

Fasten a yardstick to the edge of your workbench so it is always available for easy measuring just by holding items up against it. If you cut keyhole slots in the yardstick, it can be removed when needed elsewhere.

Repair and Repaint

Paint lines a foot apart on a concrete shop floor as an aid in measuring lumber or pipe.

Appliance-Go-Around

A Lazy Susan makes an ideal rotating work area for repairing small appliances. It allows you to get at the appliance easily from all sides.

Repair and Repaint

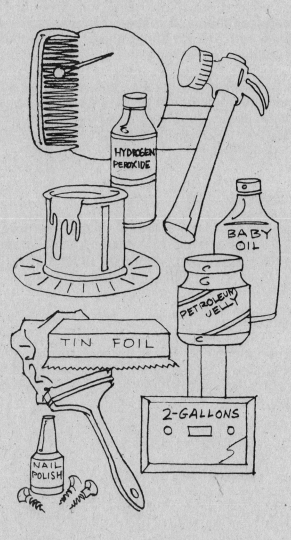

Labels in illustration: HYDROGEN PEROXIDE · BABY OIL · PETROLEUM JELLY · TIN FOIL · 2-GALLONS · NAIL POLISH

Repair and Repaint

Screwy Ideas

* A stubborn screw, bolt, or nut usually will respond to a shot of penetrating oil. If you do not have oil on hand, try hydrogen peroxide from the medicine chest or white vinegar, kerosene, or household ammonia. If these prove ineffective, heat the metal with an iron, rap it sharply with a hammer while it still is hot, and again try to loosen it.

If a bolt repeatedly loosens because of vibration, coat the threads with fingernail polish and reinstall it. It won't come loose again, but if you should have to remove it, the seal can be broken with just a little extra effort.

Change a Light Bulb

A broken light bulb can be difficult to remove because there may be little left to hold on to. Turn the switch off and jam a sponge rubber ball or large potato against the jagged glass and then turn.

Pulls and Knobs

Tighten a cabinet or dresser knob by dipping its screw or screws in fingernail polish or shellac and reinserting the knob. When the polish or shellac hardens, the screws will be set.

*WARNING: When using a flammable liquid avoid inhaling fumes by providing adequate ventilation. Never work near a flame or spark-creating flame device.

126

Bucket Brigade

A hole in a bucket can be patched several ways. If the hole isn't too large, it can be patched with candle wax. Drip melted wax over the hole from the inside of the bucket and allow it to harden. Epoxy glue can be dripped onto a crack, too.

Or use a plastic bag as a liner for the bucket; the weight of the contents inside the bucket will keep the bag in place.

If you are having difficulty finding the hole so you can patch it, turn the bucket upside down over a light. The light will shine through any holes.

Nail Down the Problem

Avoid a smashed thumb or finger when hammering a small brad, tack, or nail by slipping the fastener between the teeth of a pocket comb. The comb will hold the nail, while you hold the other end of the comb. A bobbie pin or paper clip are other satisfactory holders.

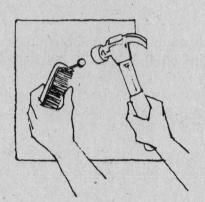

Repair and Repaint

When pulling nails with a claw hammer, protect the wall or board beneath the hammer by slipping a scrap of wood or a plastic spatula under the hammer head. The spatula will provide additional leverage, too.

By slipping the rubber tip from a crutch over the head of a hammer, you can turn it into a firm yet soft-headed mallet that will cause less damage.

A Vase Trick

If you have a vase or flower bowl that has sprung a leak, coat the inside of the container with melted paraffin. When this hardens, the container will be water-tight again.

Garden Hose

Fix a small leak in a plastic hose by barely touching it with the tip of a hot ice pick. The plastic will melt and seal the hole.

Painting

An easy way to keep paint off window panes when painting window frames is to mask the edge of the panes with tape. If you have no tape, a handy alternative is newspaper. Dampen the paper so it will temporarily adhere to the glass, and slip it off as you complete each frame.

You can mask various areas for a wall graphic with self-sticking shelf paper.

If you don't want or can't remove hinges and other hardware when painting adjacent areas, coat them with petroleum jelly before painting. If you accidentally get paint on the hardware, it then can be wiped off easily.

Drip Catcher

Glue a paper plate to the bottom of your paint can to serve as a drip catcher. The plate moves along with the can and is much more convenient than a bunch of newspapers.

Painting Tips

Enamel paint can be applied more smoothly if the can first is allowed to stand in a pan of hot water. (Be sure not to put the can near a flame; heat the water first and then remove the pan from heat.)

When painting kitchen or bathroom cabinets, finish the insides first. Also, paint the tops, bottoms, and sides before starting on the front frames and doors. If you proceed in this order, you won't have to reach over areas already painted and risk smearing them.

A pair of tweezers can be used to pick loose brush bristles off freshly painted surfaces.

If you need to leave your paint brush for a short while and don't want to clean it, keep it soft and pliable by wrapping it in foil or a plastic bag.

Put the wrapped brush in the freezer for longer periods of time.

Repair and Repaint

Before capping leftover paint, mark the label at the level of the paint inside so you can tell at a glance how much is left in the can.

Leftover paint sometimes contains hardened globs that have dropped in from the edge of the can. Strain these out by dropping a circle of window screen into the can. As the screen sinks or is pushed to the bottom of the can, the paint above will be free of imperfections.

Keep a record of how much paint it takes to cover each room by writing the amount on the back of a light switch plate. You will be removing the switch plate before you paint, anyway.

Clean Up

Remove paint splatters from your hair or skin by rubbing the paint with baby oil.

* Clean your paint brushes without ruining your hands by pouring solvent into a strong, clear plastic bag and inserting the brush. Work the solvent into the brush through the plastic, and your hands will stay clean.

After you have cleaned your brushes, dip them in a final rinse containing fabric softener. This will keep them as soft as they were when new.

Nail polish remover will take paint splatters off tile.

*WARNING: When using a flammable liquid avoid inhaling fumes by providing adequate ventilation. Never work near a flame or spark-creating flame device.

Additional Storage

Additional Storage

Clothes and Linens

New garbage cans of either metal or plastic make good storage containers for clothing. If they are airtight, you won't even need to use mothballs.

Large, metal, clean potato chip cans are suitable for storing small items of clothing.

If you are fortunate enough to have a cedar closet but it no longer smells like one, lightly sand its surfaces. The sanding will open the wood's pores and release a new cedar odor.

Remember, the cedar odor does not kill moths; it simply repels them. Clean all clothes before storage to remove any moth eggs.

Convert a closet or chest to a cedar closet or chest by installing thin cedar slats over inside surfaces.

Weatherstrip a cedar closet to contain the scent.

If you live in a humid climate and plan to pack away clothing in corrugated boxes, first coat the box with thinned shellac to keep out moisture.

When storing heirloom linens or baby clothing, don't starch or iron them. Wash and rinse them; then rinse again in a vinegar-and-water solution, and if possible allow them to dry in the sun. Finally, wrap each item separately in pale blue tissue paper, with extra paper between the folds.

Finding Extra Storage Space

Take a tip from your medicine chest if it is built

into the space between studs in your wall. If all your interior walls are constructed of studs and drywall, other similar cabinets can be added where needed. Put a liquor cabinet over your bar, for example, or fashion a canned-goods pantry in the kitchen.

A clipboard hung from a cup hook inside a cabinet or pantry door can hold placemats.

Replace a wooden step with another on hinges; the space under the hinged step can hold boots or sports equipment that otherwise would clutter the house.

Additional Storage

The inside of almost every closet door can be turned into useful storage space with the addition of hooks, shelves, or hanging bins.

Most closets can accommodate a second shelf above the existing one. If the rod is installed high enough, there might even be room for another one beneath it on which to hang shorter items such as slacks and shirts.

Don't treat your hallways as mere passageways. If they are wide enough, line them with shelves or shallow cabinets.

Suitcases are good places to stash out-of-season clothing or linens. They take up no more room filled than they do empty.

Use flat, roll-out bins for under-the-bed storage. They can hold bed linens, sewing supplies, photographs or other infrequently needed items.

To make the most of every square inch under a stairway, construct a wheeled triangular unit that fits into the farthest area under the stairs.

Home Safety

Basement Safety

Mix a little sand in with the paint when painting basement stairs so they will be less slippery.

To make basement stairs easier to see and therefore safer, edge them with luminous paint.

Light the basement with a two-socket fixture; if one bulb burns out you won't be left in the dark.

Avoiding Accidents

To avoid accidents, wipe up spilled water, grease, and other liquids from your kitchen, bathroom, and garage floors as soon as possible.

Anchor rolled up sections of carpet firmly to prevent someone from tripping.

Secure throw rugs with nonskid pads and don't use them at the top or bottom of a flight of stairs.

If you staple burlap to the bottom step of a ladder, you'll have a scraper for your shoes. This way you won't have any slippery substances left on your shoes.

If someone in the family frequently gets out of bed in the middle of the night, paint door edges with luminous paint to help that person avoid running into the door in the dark.

To prevent grease fires, keep the stove clear of pot holders, paper napkins, and towels when frying food.

Security Measures

Ask your neighbors to use your garbage cans when you're on vacation, so your absence won't be so evident.

Safeguard your home by not leaving notes for workmen or family members on the door.

If you're going to be away from home for several days—or even for just one day—adjust your telephone ring to its lowest volume. To a prowler, an unanswered phone is a quick tip that your home is empty.

Arrange to have newspaper delivery stopped when you're away from home, and have a neighbor pick up your mail.

Let neighbors know of any suspicious-looking person or strange cars you notice lurking about.

Keep your curtains drawn or remove valuables to rooms where they can't be seen from outside.

To prevent burglars from stealing ladders stored outdoors, padlock them to something that cannot be moved.

To keep your tools from being stolen, paint the handles. Thieves avoid items that are easy to identify.

For the most effective alarm system, conceal all wiring. A burglar looks for places where he can disconnect the security system.

A door with too much space between the door and the frame is an invitation for the burglar to use a jimmy. Reinforce such a door by attaching a panel of ¾-inch plywood or a piece of sheet metal to it.

If there are door hinges on the outside of your house, take down the door and reset the hinges inside. Otherwise all a thief has to do to gain entry to your home is knock out the hinge pin.

You can burglar-proof your glass patio doors by setting a pipe or metal bar in the inside bottom track of the door slide. The pipe should be the same length as the track.

It's easy for a burglar to pry his way through rot, so replace rotted door frames with new, solid wood.

It's simple for a thief to break glass panels and then reach in and open a doorknob from the inside. A door with glass panels should be either fortified or replaced.

Ask for credentials from any salesman who requests entry to your home—even security system salesmen. Many professional burglars use this cover to check out homes. If you want to buy an electronic alarm system, make your own contacts with reputable firms.

Protect your windows with one or more good locks, an alarm system, burglar-resistant glass, or many small panes instead of one large area of glass.

In a rented house, install a double cylinder lock that requires a key to open it from the inside as well as from the outside. If a thief breaks through the panel and reaches in, he still has the lock to deal with instead of just a knob.

Protecting Your Valuables

If you don't have a safe, or feel you don't need one, find good hiding places for your valuables in your home. An acoustical tile ceiling offers good hiding possibilities. Remove a tile and restore it afterwards with magnetic fastener or a similar device. However, be careful not to leave finger marks.

You can keep your jewelry safe by installing a wall-outlet safe. When the safe is closed, it looks just like an electrical outlet. When buying a wall safe, be sure it's fireproof as well as burglar-proof.

A chiseled-out space in the top of a door makes a great "safe" for small valuables. Or you might devise a hiding place in a false ceiling.

Fireplace logs can be hollowed out to make hiding places, too. Other ideas include the underside of desktops, linings of drapes, underneath insulation in the attic, inside a lamp. Avoid the obvious places such as mattresses, drawers, inside figurines, behind pictures, and under carpets.

Garage Management

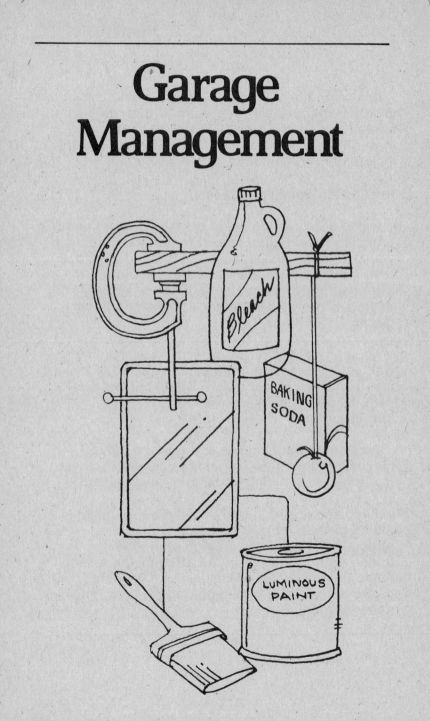

Oil and Grease Stains

Oil and grease spots on the garage floor or driveway should be cleaned off as soon as possible.

Lift an oil spot with baking soda.

Cornmeal also will absorb stains.

* To clean such spots, apply paint thinner and then cover overnight with an absorbent substance, such as cat litter, dry Portland cement, or sand.

* A degreasing compound can be substituted for paint thinner. It can be purchased in either liquid or aerosol form at an auto supply store.

As a last resort, try removing a stain from concrete with full-strength laundry bleach.

Protecting the Garage Floor

Protect your garage floor by using a drip pan under the car. Fashion a pan from a cookie sheet filled with a layer of cat litter to absorb drips. Replace the cat litter when it becomes saturated.

Or, cut a piece of corrugated cardboard to fit the pan, and change it when necessary.

If you need a drip pan larger than a cookie sheet, make one out of aluminum foil stapled to a piece of corrugated cardboard.

*WARNING: When using a flammable liquid avoid inhaling fumes by providing adequate ventilation. Never work near a flame or spark-creating flame device.

Garage Management

Camouflage car drippings on the garage floor by painting a wide black stripe on it the width of the space between the car's tires. This stripe can serve as a parking guide, too.

Put a door mat in the entry from an attached garage to the house to prevent people from tracking in oil or grease.

Parking

Install a bumper guard on the end garage wall so you won't hit the wall itself. Fashion a simple guard by hanging an old tire on the wall at the height of your bumper.

As a guide for parking your car in the garage, suspend a ball on a string from the ceiling. Properly park your car and then hang the ball so it almost touches the windshield at the driver's eye level. Now, when you drive in, use the ball to guide you to a stop just before the windshield touches the ball and you'll never hit the end of the garage.

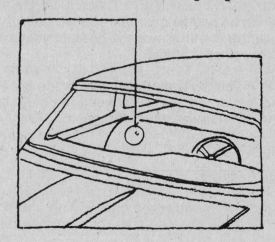

Paint luminous stripes on the end garage wall as a parking guide.

Paint white lines on the garage floor to outline parking spaces for bicycles, the lawn mower, and other large objects so they never will be in the way of the car.

Sections of inner tube attached to the sides of the garage entry will help keep you from scratching your car when parking.

Also protect your car doors by stapling inner tube sections, foam rubber, carpet or upholstery scraps, or rubber mats to the side walls where open doors might hit.

Garage Storage

To maximize floor space in a garage, hang as many items as possible on the walls.

Shelves or cabinets can fill the top half of the garage's front wall, since the hood of your car doesn't require that space.

Also, if you lay a platform across the garage ceiling joists, the space between the ceiling and the roof can be used for storage.

Garage Security

If you have an attached garage with a door that lifts on a track, you can give your house added

security at night by tightening a C-clamp on the
track next to a roller. The door cannot be opened
with the clamp in place.

Install a door viewer in the door between the
house and the attached garage so if you hear a
noise in the garage, you can check without opening
the door.

The Yard

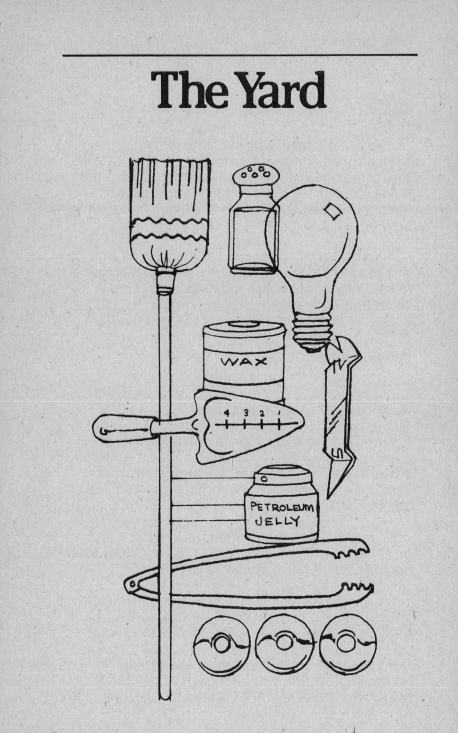

The Yard

Lights

If you install new light bulbs outdoors at the beginning of winter you probably won't have to do this chore again during cold weather. Should the bulbs you remove still have life in them, install them indoors or save them to reinstall outdoors in spring.

A light coat of petroleum jelly rubbed on the threads of outdoor light bulbs will help keep out moisture and make the bulbs easier to remove when they burn out.

Patio Furniture

Wicker outdoor furniture can be cleaned with warm salt water and a stiff brush.

When storing folding patio chairs, slip an old pillow case over each end of a chair and tape the cases together. The fabric will protect against scratches and dirt but will not trap moisture, as plastic bags might.

Keep moisture from harming your patio furniture's cushions by using a plastic pillow cover under the decorative cushion covering.

If you wax the bottoms of the legs on wooden patio furniture, you will keep out moisture. The furniture will be easier on the patio floor, too.

If you insert metal washers in the protective rubber cups on the legs of tubular metal patio chairs, the metal will not cut through the tips.

Drill holes in the seats of metal patio furniture so rain water can drain out. If water is allowed to collect, the seats will rust.

Stepping Stones

Instead of using conventional stepping stones, make your walk a trip down memory lane. Have each member of the family put his hand prints, name, and birth date in a square of wet cement, and mark other important dates in remaining squares.

Barbecues

Keep an empty plastic squeeze bottle by the barbecue grill to use as a bellows on the coals.

Turn an old barbecue grill into a conversation piece. Paint it, fill it with soil, and plant flowers or vines in it.

Frost-Free Locks

Wrap outdoor padlocks with plastic sandwich bags during the winter to keep them from freezing.

Plant Life

Save your hands when pruning prickly branches by using barbecue tongs to hold the greenery.

Use blobs of putty with wires embedded in them to hold vines you want to climb on brick or masonry walls. The putty will stick to the wall and the wire will hold the vine.

The Yard

Keep weeds from growing in the cracks of your walks or driveway by dousing the cracks with salt.

If you mark off inches on your garden trowel or shovel, you will have a handy guide for planting seeds and bulbs at the right depth.

When you dig a hole to plant a large bush or tree, pile the soil from the hole on a large piece of plastic laid out next to the hole. Once the plant is in place, lift the plastic and the soil will slide back into the hole.

When moving a heavy rock, plant, or sack of fertilizer, slide the heavy object onto a piece of carpet to pull it along.

Moving

Moving

Planning a Move

Make a master check list of everything that has to be done in connection with the move, and try to make a schedule noting deadlines for each task.

Hold a garage sale to dispose of unwanted items. You will make some money and also save by not having to pay for moving useless possessions.

Try not to overlook anyone when notifying people about your move. Include utilities, post office, social security, publications to which you subscribe, insurance companies and phone company.

Packing

Use inexpensive, new plastic garbage cans as "boxes" for breakables. Later, those not needed for garbage will make vermin-proof, watertight storage containers.

Use small linens such as towels, washcloths, and pillow cases as packing material for dishes. They protect the dishes and don't waste space.

To minimize breakage of glass items, pack the heavier ones at the bottom with the more delicate pieces on top.

Stand plates on edge when packing them; they'll be less likely to break.

If you have several days in which to pack before moving, dampen excelsior so it will shape itself to the china and dishes.

Pack books so their spines are alternated.

It may be cheaper to ship books via the United States mail than to send them in the moving van. The Post Office offers an inexpensive, 4th-class book rate.

Put all screws, brackets, and hardware into plastic sandwich or garbage bags and then staple or tape them to the furnishings they belong with.

Tape the hook for each picture to the pack of the picture.

Furniture casters sometimes fall out when a piece is lifted. Remove them ahead of time, and use heavy twine to keep them together. Tag them so you know which piece they fit.

Taping lightly loaded bureau drawers in place with wide masking tape saves packing the drawer's contents. Remove the tape as soon as the furniture arrives to minimize tape marks.

Moving

To prevent odors from developing in the refrigerator or freezer during the move, put several charcoal briquets inside the unit to absorb them.

Or, fill the box with wads of newspapers. The paper will absorb any moisture and prevent odors.

When You Arrive

Take a "care" package along with the family so you can survive until the van arrives. Include instant coffee, cups, spoons, soap and towels, a can and bottle opener, a few light bulbs, a flashlight, toilet paper, cleansing powder, and a first aid kit.

Be sure daily medications travel with you, not the movers.

It's nice to have a clock, radio, and maybe even a portable TV at your new home if you are going to arrive before the movers.

At the New Place

Draw a floor plan of the new home and sketch in and number your furnishings as they will be arranged. Then tag the actual furniture pieces, and the movers will know where to put each one.

If you have access to the new home a day or so before the moving van arrives, set off a bug bomb or spray. (Even if you don't see bugs, there probably are some.) This way, there are no people or foods to worry about during the spraying.

Cars

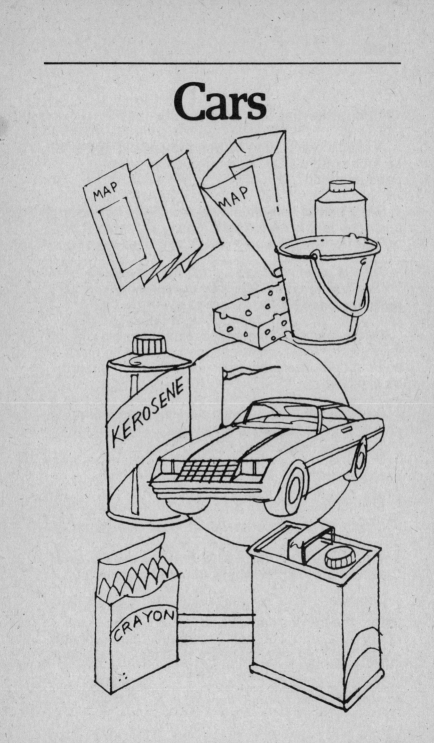

Cleaning the Car

A child's crayon can be used to camouflage small scratches if you can match the color on your car's paint job.

* Mix a pint of kerosene into a gallon of hot water and sponge this on to clean your car. The solution takes off even stubborn road film and leaves a waxy finish.

Carpet scraps make good car scrubbers and polishing pads.

Soften a stiff chamois by soaking it in a gallon of warm water to which a teaspoon of olive oil has been added. After about fifteen minutes, it should be like new.

Crumpled foil can be used to clean and shine your bumper or other chrome.

Don't wash or wax your car in direct sunlight or even when the finish is still hot from the sun.

A vegetable brush is a good tool for cleaning the grillwork on your car.

Leftover tea will clean road film from your windshield and head lights.

Use nylon net to scrub insects off the windshield and chrome.

Dip a wet sponge in baking soda to remove insects without scratching the car finish.

*WARNING: When using a flammable liquid avoid inhaling fumes by providing adequate ventilation. Never work near a flame or spark-creating flame device.

Machine oil will remove tar from a car bumper. Apply the oil, allow it to work a few moments to soften the tar, and the tar can be wiped away. Linseed oil also will soften tar.

A coat of liquid shoe polish will protect rubber auto floor mats and make them look shiny and new.

Making It Easy

The car antenna will go up and down easier if you occasionally rub it with wax paper.

When you'll be parked for an hour or so in possible ice or snow conditions, rub a slice of onion over your windshield. The glass will remain fairly clear, and any precipitation that does stick can easily be scraped off.

Fogged car windows can be cleaned with a blackboard eraser.

If the lock on your car freezes, heat the key over a flame and work it into the lock. It may take several tries, but you'll get into the car.

Sand can supply needed traction on snow or ice when sprinkled under your car's drive wheels. Carry a small supply in the trunk during the winter. A small bag of commercial cat litter is a convenient substitute for sand.

Floor mats placed under the drive wheels sometimes are effective in supplying traction, too.

Travel Tips

Never carry a spare can of gasoline in your car; it could explode. However, an empty, clean can could be useful if you run out of gas and must walk to a gas station.

* When you are pouring gasoline from a can that has no spout, make a funnel from a road map or a piece of aluminum foil.

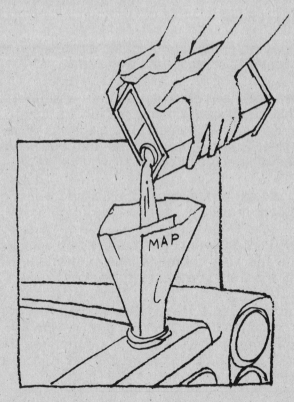

*WARNING: When using a flammable liquid avoid inhaling fumes by providing adequate ventilation. Never work near a flame or spark-creating flame device.

If you're going to have to get your hands greasy when working under the hood, rub a thin coat of petroleum jelly over your hands before you start so grease can't get into the pores. Cleaning up will be easier.

Shaving cream can be used as an on-the-road cleaner for dirty hands.

Keep change for an emergency phone call under the floor mat or in some other handy hiding place.

If you ever need water for your radiator and have no container, maybe a hubcap can be used.

Use a barbecue cook's glove when you have to touch hot parts under the hood.

Protect the ball on a trailer hitch by slipping a slit tennis ball over it. The cover keeps out moisture.

Traveling

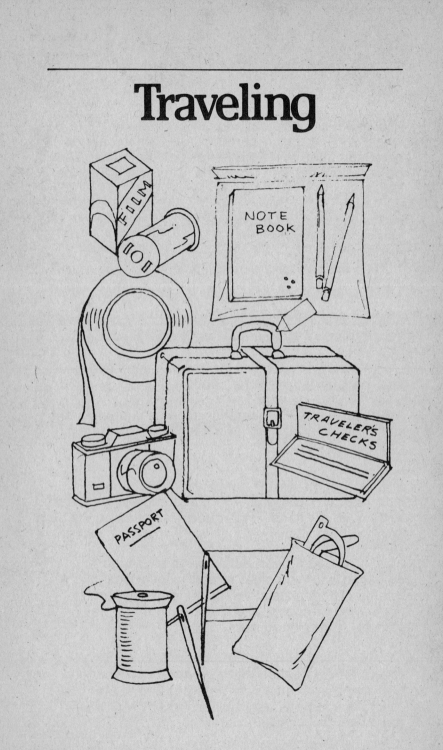

Packing for a Trip

Label luggage inside as well as outside with your name and address.

As you pack, make a detailed list describing the contents of each bag. The list will make it easier for the carrier to track down lost luggage and also will help with an insurance claim. Carry the list with you.

Put heavy items such as shoes in the bottom of the suitcase next to the hinges.

Stuff socks and other small, soft articles into your shoes and purses.

Items such as lingerie, underwear, and socks travel and pack better when they are rolled.

Camera and Films

Don't permit airport security x-ray scanners to ruin your film. Carry your film and camera with you and insist on "hand" inspection. FAA regulations give you that right.

When traveling abroad, leave your camera unloaded until you clear airport inspections. Many foreign officials insist on machine inspection for concealed weapons, and if you have film in the camera, it may be ruined.

If you travel outside the United States with a recent model camera and expensive accessories, fill out a customs form prior to departure. Doing so can save you time, aggravation, and money when you return through U.S. customs.

Traveling

If you remove belts from slacks and pack them around the edge of the case, you will better utilize the space.

Health and Comfort

You'll have few problems with your prescription drugs if they travel in their original containers. Take along a copy of the prescription for any medication that might raise the eyebrows of a law enforcement officer.

If you are dependent upon your eyeglasses, carry a spare pair with you any time you travel abroad. In the United States, carry a copy of your prescription with you.

Air Travel

If your checked luggage does not arrive with you, report the loss to the airline before you leave the airport and keep a copy of the form you fill out.

The airline should pay the cost of delivering your lost luggage to your home or hotel, rental fees for missing sporting equipment, and a portion of the cost of replacing clothing and toiletries.